Juke Joint JUMBLE®

Puzzles That Shake, Rattle, and Roll!

Henri Arnold, Bob Lee, and Mike Argirion

TRIUMPH
BOOKS

This book is available in quantity at special discounts
for your group or organization.

For further information, contact:

Triumph Books
542 South Dearborn Street
Suite 750
Chicago, Illinois 60605
(312) 939-3330
Fax (312) 663-3557
www.triumphbooks.com

Printed in U.S.A.

ISBN: 978-1-60078-295-4

Design by Sue Knopf

CONTENTS

Juke Joint
JUMBLE®

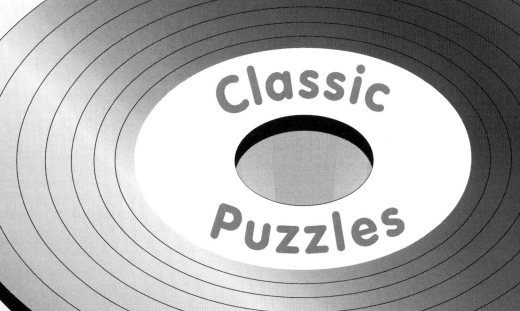

Classic

Puzzles

JUMBLE®

Unscramble these four Jumbles, one letter to each square, to form four ordinary words.

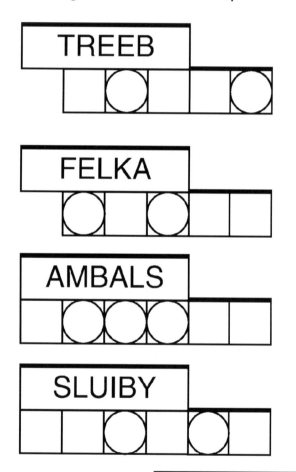

TREEB

FELKA

AMBALS

SLUIBY

Another one?

Forget it! I'm going home

PTOOEY

STALE BEER CAN LEAD TO THIS.

Now arrange the circled letters to form the surprise answer, as suggested by the above cartoon.

Print answer here " ⬡⬡⬡⬡ " ⬡⬡⬡⬡⬡

JUMBLE®

Unscramble these four Jumbles, one letter to each square, to form four ordinary words.

AMGUT

TULSY

ZERTHI

REPJUM

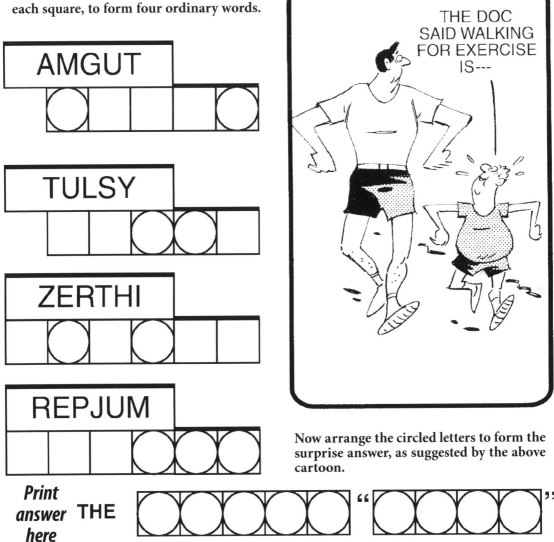

THE DOC SAID WALKING FOR EXERCISE IS---

Now arrange the circled letters to form the surprise answer, as suggested by the above cartoon.

Print answer here   THE ◯◯◯◯◯◯ " ◯◯◯◯ "

JUMBLE®

Unscramble these four Jumbles, one letter to each square, to form four ordinary words.

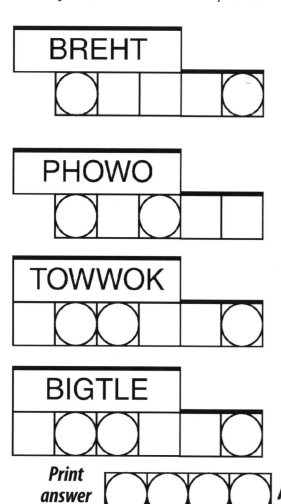

BREHT

PHOWO

TOWWOK

BIGTLE

Tie your fancy ribbon, and voilà!

HOW SHE FINISHED HER GIFT-WRAPPING DEMONSTRATION.

Now arrange the circled letters to form the surprise answer, as suggested by the above cartoon.

Print answer here   A

JUMBLE

Unscramble these four Jumbles, one letter to each square, to form four ordinary words.

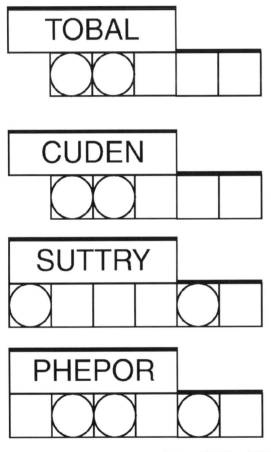

TOBAL

CUDEN

SUTTRY

PHEPOR

Sorry, nothing I can do

HONK! HONK!

WHEN THE SODA TRUCK STALLED, TRAFFIC WAS---

Now arrange the circled letters to form the surprise answer, as suggested by the above cartoon.

Print answer here "◯◯◯◯◯◯◯" ◯◯

JUMBLE®

Unscramble these four Jumbles, one letter to each square, to form four ordinary words.

EUQER

ANCKK

BOLIFE

SWUNIE

$50,000 in prizes

He's got a good ride going

WHAT THE BRONCO RIDER ENDED UP GETTING IN THE RODEO.

Now arrange the circled letters to form the surprise answer, as suggested by the above cartoon.

Print answer here A ◯◯◯ " ◯◯◯◯◯◯ "

JUMBLE

Unscramble these four Jumbles, one letter to
each square, to form four ordinary words.

TALEV

HINKT

MUCAUV

GUAJAR

Good
shot

He even
looks the
part

WHEN THE POOL
HUSTLER APPEARED
ON THE MOVIE
SET, HE WAS----

Now arrange the circled letters to form the
surprise answer, as suggested by the above
cartoon.

Print answer here ◯◯◯◯◯ ON " ◯◯◯ "

7

JUMBLE®

Unscramble these four Jumbles, one letter to each square, to form four ordinary words.

TALAN

YONIS

PHILSO

WALUTO

You're going places, m'boy

LOBBY

HE RODE THE EXECUTIVE ELE-VATOR BECAUSE HE WAS——

Now arrange the circled letters to form the surprise answer, as suggested by the above cartoon.

Print answer here ◯◯ ◯◯◯ ◯◯◯ "◯◯"

8

JUMBLE®

Unscramble these four Jumbles, one letter to each square, to form four ordinary words.

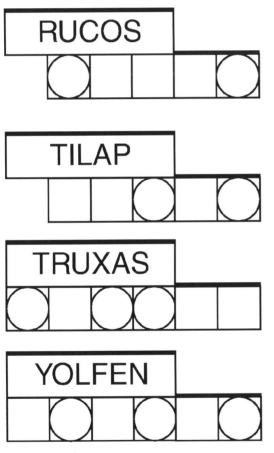

RUCOS

TILAP

TRUXAS

YOLFEN

You're grounded for a week

It won't happen again

WHEN HE APOLO-
GIZED FOR MISSING
CURFEW, HE WAS
IN A ----

Now arrange the circled letters to form the surprise answer, as suggested by the above cartoon.

Print answer here " ◯◯◯◯◯ " ◯◯◯◯◯

JUMBLE

Unscramble these four Jumbles, one letter to each square, to form four ordinary words.

TOYBO

UGGEA

VOICEN

CAMEEN

He's got great rhythm

WHAT HE TURNED INTO AT THE MASKED BALL.

Now arrange the circled letters to form the surprise answer, as suggested by the above cartoon.

Print answer here

A " ⬡⬡⬡⬡⬡⬡ " ⬡⬡⬡

Unscramble these four Jumbles, one letter to each square, to form four ordinary words.

HEALT

LOVEC

YAMFIL

BESPIC

I can't keep up

He's become famous

WHEN THE HAIR-DRESSER APPEARED ON TV, HIS BUSI-NESS GREW AT A----

Now arrange the circled letters to form the surprise answer, as suggested by the above cartoon.

Print answer here " "

JUMBLE®

Unscramble these four Jumbles, one letter to each square, to form four ordinary words.

EUQUE

UNPER

BLAVER

DOLSUN

No! No! That's only for hot dogs!

WHEN HE TOPPED THE ICE CREAM WITH HOT CHILI SAUCE, THE SODA JERK SAID----

Now arrange the circled letters to form the surprise answer, as suggested by the above cartoon.

Print answer here "◯◯◯◯◯ ON ◯◯◯◯◯◯"

JUMBLE®

Unscramble these four Jumbles, one letter to each square, to form four ordinary words.

NUSEE

EFTUL

SMIDOW

KOTLEC

You cut me off

Why don't you learn how to drive!

ROAD RAGE CAN MAKE THIS COME TO A HEAD.

Now arrange the circled letters to form the surprise answer, as suggested by the above cartoon.

Print answer here **A** ☐☐☐☐ **OR** ☐☐☐

JUMBLE®

Unscramble these four Jumbles, one letter to each square, to form four ordinary words.

JYTET

HYNIS

NARIFA

LEMITY

Yea
yea

WHEN THEIR
TEAM LOST, THE
FANS WERE----

Now arrange the circled letters to form the surprise answer, as suggested by the above cartoon.

Print answer here

JUMBLE®

Unscramble these four Jumbles, one letter to
each square, to form four ordinary words.

DYNBA

AKQUE

RIVETH

YEWARL

I love
your new
style

Brunette's my
natural color

She's older
than she
looks

SHE DYED HER
HAIR BECAUSE
IT HELPED
KEEP HER AGE----

Now arrange the circled letters to form the
surprise answer, as suggested by the above
cartoon.

Print
answer
here

"   "

15

JUMBLE®

Unscramble these four Jumbles, one letter to each square, to form four ordinary words.

UPTYT

KECHO

MABOOB

SMIBUT

RECRUITING OFFICE

WHERE THE SHOE-MAKER ENDED UP WHEN HE JOINED THE MARINES.

Now arrange the circled letters to form the surprise answer, as suggested by the above cartoon.

Print answer here IN " ☐ " ☐

JUMBLE®

Unscramble these four Jumbles, one letter to each square, to form four ordinary words.

SOYUM

TENFO

KOPHOU

WALCOL

She's been practicing for weeks

WHAT IT TAKES A HARPIST TO PLAY BEFORE AN AUDIENCE.

Now arrange the circled letters to form the surprise answer, as suggested by the above cartoon.

Print answer here ⬡⬡⬡⬡ OF ⬡⬡⬡⬡⬡

JUMBLE®

Unscramble these four Jumbles, one letter to
each square, to form four ordinary words.

INNEL

SCEHS

NOPPIL

GLEIMN

I hear
Alice and
Horace
were seen...

WHAT A COUPLE
OF BUSYBODIES
ARE GOOD AT
FEEDING.

Now arrange the circled letters to form the
surprise answer, as suggested by the above
cartoon.

Print
answer THE
here

JUMBLE

Unscramble these four Jumbles, one letter to
each square, to form four ordinary words.

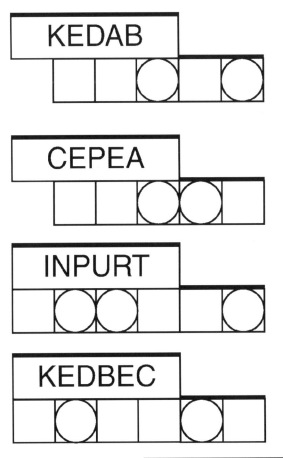

KEDAB

CEPEA

INPURT

KEDBEC

You're so clumsy

Ha ha ha

WHEN HE DROPPED
THE CARTON OF
EGGS, HIS
COWORKERS----

Now arrange the circled letters to form the
surprise answer, as suggested by the above
cartoon.

Print answer here " ⬡⬡⬡⬡⬡⬡⬡ " ⬡⬡

19

JUMBLE

Unscramble these four Jumbles, one letter to
each square, to form four ordinary words.

CHARN

DEWEG

YARREL

VILDER

Are you
sure you
can fix it?

A
snap

WHAT HUBBY DID
WHEN THE CEIL-
ING FAN NEEDED
REPAIR.

Now arrange the circled letters to form the
surprise answer, as suggested by the above
cartoon.

Print
answer
here

IT A

20

JUMBLE®

Unscramble these four Jumbles, one letter to each square, to form four ordinary words.

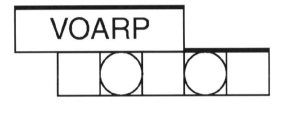

VOARP

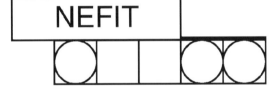

NEFIT

COSHUR

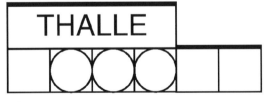

THALLE

To our good friend Jacque

ENJOYED AT THE PARIS EATERY.

Now arrange the circled letters to form the surprise answer, as suggested by the above cartoon.

Print answer here

" "

JUMBLE®

Unscramble these four Jumbles, one letter to each square, to form four ordinary words.

TCHAB

WOSNO

DARZAH

YOWHLL

Who, me?

WHEN JUNIOR SAID HE DIDN'T SNEAK A COOKIE, MOM FOUND IT WAS----

Now arrange the circled letters to form the surprise answer, as suggested by the above cartoon.

Print answer here

☐☐☐☐ TO ☐☐☐☐☐☐☐☐☐

JUMBLE®

Unscramble these four Jumbles, one letter to each square, to form four ordinary words.

VOYNE

NALST

DANCEN

ANIZIN

Guess I shouldn't get involved with those guys

THE GAMBLER WHO WENT BROKE LACKED THIS.

Now arrange the circled letters to form the surprise answer, as suggested by the above cartoon.

Print answer here "◯◯◯◯◯◯◯◯"

23

JUMBLE®

Unscramble these four Jumbles, one letter to each square, to form four ordinary words.

ELLIS

CARPH

GLIJEN

THARRE

This is fantastic. What a thrill

WHAT HE EXPERI-ENCED IN THE LOW PART OF THE OCEAN.

Now arrange the circled letters to form the surprise answer, as suggested by the above cartoon.

Print answer here A ⬡⬡⬡⬡⬡ " ⬡⬡⬡⬡⬡ "

JUMBLE®

Unscramble these four Jumbles, one letter to each square, to form four ordinary words.

VABER

CUIJY

DORRAM

MARSID

That's it 'til next year

HOW MOM FELT AFTER MAKING JAM.

Now arrange the circled letters to form the surprise answer, as suggested by the above cartoon.

Print answer here " ⬡⬡⬡⬡⬡⬡ "

25

JUMBLE.

Unscramble these four Jumbles, one letter to each square, to form four ordinary words.

CEPIE

YADEC

DEBOHL

CLARIA

WHAT HE CON-
SIDERED THE
LOVELY VENDOR.

Now arrange the circled letters to form the surprise answer, as suggested by the above cartoon.

Print answer here A ⬡⬡⬡⬡⬡ " ⬡⬡⬡⬡⬡⬡ "

JUMBLE®

Unscramble these four Jumbles, one letter to each square, to form four ordinary words.

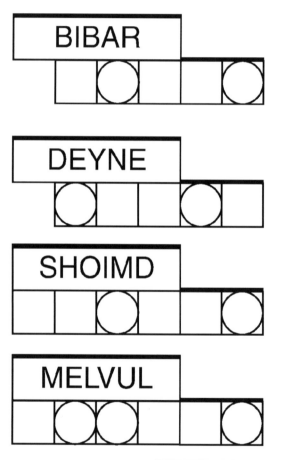

BIBAR

DEYNE

SHOIMD

MELVUL

Sally's on cloud nine

He's a good catch

WHEN THE WOMAN PILOT GOT MAR-RIED, HER FRIENDS SAID SHE---

Now arrange the circled letters to form the surprise answer, as suggested by the above cartoon.

Print answer here " ◯◯◯◯◯◯ " ◯◯◯

JUMBLE®

Unscramble these four Jumbles, one letter to each square, to form four ordinary words.

BAIDE

LYMAN

NATTYR

PULCEO

There should be plenty of guys on board

WHAT SHE HOPED TO MEET ON THE SINGLES CRUISE.

Now arrange the circled letters to form the surprise answer, as suggested by the above cartoon.

Print answer here A " ◯◯◯◯◯◯◯◯◯◯ "

JUMBLE®

Unscramble these four Jumbles, one letter to each square, to form four ordinary words.

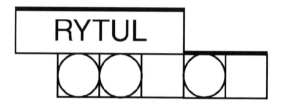

RYTUL

NOROH

LINOCU

TRYGEN

Just two grams of fat

High in fiber, low in fat

PRACTICED BY THE DIETING COUPLE.

Now arrange the circled letters to form the surprise answer, as suggested by the above cartoon.

Print answer here " ⃝⃝⃝⃝⃝ " ⃝⃝⃝⃝⃝⃝⃝

PUZZLE
29

JUMBLE®

Unscramble these four Jumbles, one letter to each square, to form four ordinary words.

CYDER

THYFE

CLIPES

HIRTHE

It's a gusher, Sam

We're in the bucks

WHEN THE WILD-CATTERS STRUCK OIL, THEY ENDED UP----

Now arrange the circled letters to form the surprise answer, as suggested by the above cartoon.

Print answer here ⬡⬡⬡⬡⬡⬡ , ⬡⬡⬡⬡

31

JUMBLE®

Unscramble these four Jumbles, one letter to each square, to form four ordinary words.

SUMIC

DOFOL

YAIMDS

PHORTY

Alice, you've been in there forever

WHAT THE SHOWER TURNED INTO WHEN SHE TOOK TOO MUCH TIME.

Now arrange the circled letters to form the surprise answer, as suggested by the above cartoon.

Print answer here A

JUMBLE®

Unscramble these four Jumbles, one letter to
each square, to form four ordinary words.

TIARE

LUNCE

GESTAK

CHUROC

Everything
balances,
your
majesty

THE REVIEW OF
ROYAL FINANCES
TURNED OUT TO
BE A----

Now arrange the circled letters to form the
surprise answer, as suggested by the above
cartoon.

Print " ◯◯◯◯◯ " ◯◯◯◯◯
answer
here

33

JUMBLE®

Unscramble these four Jumbles, one letter to
each square, to form four ordinary words.

FRASC

HASAW

RHODIA

KNEALT

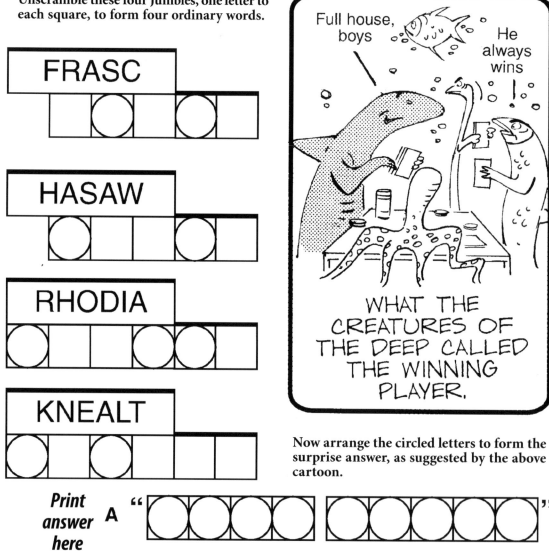

Full house,
boys

He
always
wins

WHAT THE
CREATURES OF
THE DEEP CALLED
THE WINNING
PLAYER.

Now arrange the circled letters to form the
surprise answer, as suggested by the above
cartoon.

*Print
answer
here* A " ◯◯◯◯ ◯◯◯◯◯ "

JUMBLE®

Unscramble these four Jumbles, one letter to each square, to form four ordinary words.

DYPET

ROAPE

RUMMRU

BYDOON

They come from a bigger school

THE MATH TEAM LOST THE COMPE-TITION BECAUSE THEY WERE---

Now arrange the circled letters to form the surprise answer, as suggested by the above cartoon.

Print answer here " "

JUMBLE®

Unscramble these four Jumbles, one letter to each square, to form four ordinary words.

IXTYS

FASHE

ENDTOE

SAURES

It was this big and weighed at least...

WHEN HE TOLD THEM ABOUT THE WHOPPER, HIS PALS SAID IT---

Now arrange the circled letters to form the surprise answer, as suggested by the above cartoon.

Print answer here " ⃝⃝⃝⃝⃝⃝ ⃝⃝⃝⃝⃝ "

JUMBLE®

Unscramble these four Jumbles, one letter to each square, to form four ordinary words.

BABEY

DONSY

LENZOZ

GIZHAN

Great! Now what'll we feed our family and guests?

WHAT MOM DID WHEN DAD BURNED THE STEAKS.

Now arrange the circled letters to form the surprise answer, as suggested by the above cartoon.

Print answer here " ◯◯◯◯◯◯◯ "

JUMBLE®

Unscramble these four Jumbles, one letter to each square, to form four ordinary words.

DICAR

NESOO

ONSWID

TOMSED

I just ran out of gas

HE FINISHED THIRD IN THE RACE BECAUSE HE COULDN'T GET HIS---

Now arrange the circled letters to form the surprise answer, as suggested by the above cartoon.

Print answer here " ⬡⬡⬡⬡⬡⬡ " ⬡⬡⬡⬡

JUMBLE®

Unscramble these four Jumbles, one letter to each square, to form four ordinary words.

THACC

HELEC

ANSTUE

LAFTES

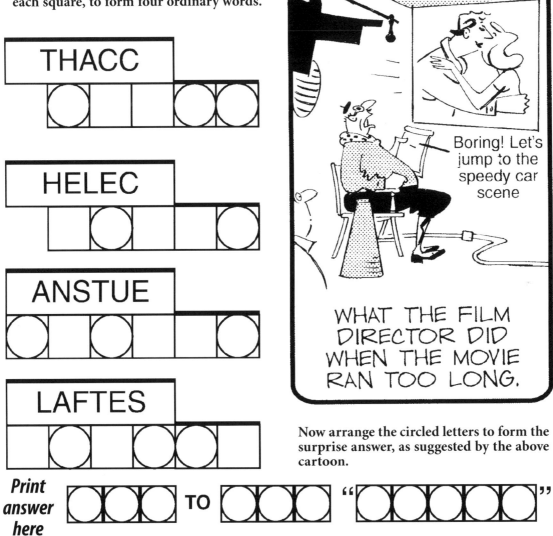

Boring! Let's jump to the speedy car scene

WHAT THE FILM DIRECTOR DID WHEN THE MOVIE RAN TOO LONG.

Now arrange the circled letters to form the surprise answer, as suggested by the above cartoon.

Print answer here ◯◯◯ TO ◯◯◯ "◯◯◯◯◯"

JUMBLE®

Unscramble these four Jumbles, one letter to each square, to form four ordinary words.

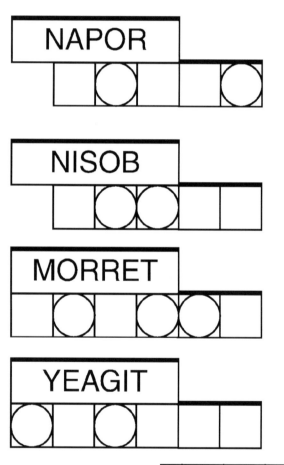

NAPOR

NISOB

MORRET

YEAGIT

After baseball, it'll be done in three hours. Guaranteed!

WHEN THE TEEN OUTLINED HIS HOMEWORK PLANS, MOM THOUGHT IT WAS---

Now arrange the circled letters to form the surprise answer, as suggested by the above cartoon.

Print answer here " ⬡⬡⬡⬡⬡⬡⬡⬡⬡ "

40

JUMBLE

Unscramble these four Jumbles, one letter to each square, to form four ordinary words.

CNOTH

NAISE

TIMCAP

SMIREY

That "#$%&!! cut me off!

THE LOSING STOCK-CAR DRIVER WAS FINED FOR THIS.

Now arrange the circled letters to form the surprise answer, as suggested by the above cartoon.

Print answer here "☐☐☐☐☐" ☐☐☐☐☐☐☐☐☐

JUMBLE®

Unscramble these four Jumbles, one letter to each square, to form four ordinary words.

HEMTY

UNFYN

GLINTE

FARINU

Knock it off!

WOOF! WOOF!

What's wrong with him?

WHAT THE FAM-
ILY EXPERIENCED
WHEN THE BARK-
ING DOG KEPT
THEM AWAKE.

Now arrange the circled letters to form the surprise answer, as suggested by the above cartoon.

Print answer here A "⬭⬭⬭⬭" ⬭⬭⬭⬭⬭

JUMBLE®

Unscramble these four Jumbles, one letter to
each square, to form four ordinary words.

GELBI

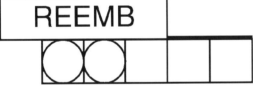

REEMB

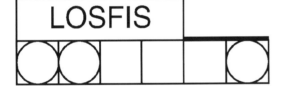

LOSFIS

RELDEG

I'm going to be like her—
pretty, smart, and popular

SHE FOLLOWED IN
THE COVER GIRL'S
FOOTSTEPS
BECAUSE SHE
WANTED----

Now arrange the circled letters to form the
surprise answer, as suggested by the above
cartoon.

Print
answer A " ◯◯◯◯◯ " ◯◯◯◯
here

JUMBLE®

Unscramble these four Jumbles, one letter to
each square, to form four ordinary words.

SHOIT

GLUNE

NIPICC

HUHRTS

C'mon, we're falling behind

Where's
my
order?

WHY THE HEAD-
WAITER HELPED
OUT IN THE
BUSY KITCHEN.

Now arrange the circled letters to form the
surprise answer, as suggested by the above
cartoon.

*Print
answer
here* TO

44

JUMBLE®

Unscramble these four Jumbles, one letter to each square, to form four ordinary words.

TURET

LERED

FARITY

MYSLOB

To the Honorable James A...

Your limo is waiting

WHAT THE TUXEDO-CLAD EXECUTIVE DICTATED TO HIS SECRETARY.

Now arrange the circled letters to form the surprise answer, as suggested by the above cartoon.

Print answer here

A "◯◯◯◯◯◯◯" ◯◯◯◯◯◯◯

JUMBLE®

Unscramble these four Jumbles, one letter to
each square, to form four ordinary words.

PLONY

MEPOT

HADEBE

TIMLEG

Stop that! Get in
here right now!

WHEN THE YOUNG
KANGAROOS MISBE-
HAVED, MOM WAS---

Now arrange the circled letters to form the
surprise answer, as suggested by the above
cartoon.

Print
answer
here

" _____ " ___

JUMBLE®

Unscramble these four Jumbles, one letter to
each square, to form four ordinary words.

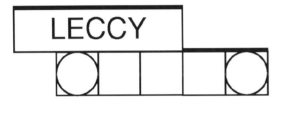

LECCY

RUYLS

VASHIL

LISHEC

We should be
selling scarves

SUN
GLASSES
$10

A COLD SNAP CAN
DO THIS TO A
BEACH VENDOR.

Now arrange the circled letters to form the
surprise answer, as suggested by the above
cartoon.

Print
answer
here   " "

JUMBLE®

Unscramble these four Jumbles, one letter to each square, to form four ordinary words.

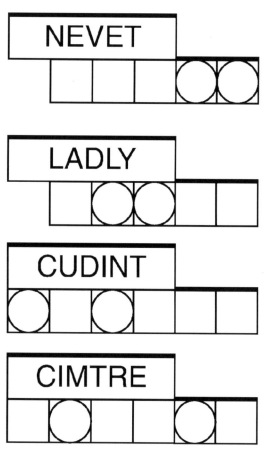

NEVET

LADLY

CUDINT

CIMTRE

Best I've seen in years

Wow!

WHAT THE CAR-
PENTER DID WHEN
HE ENTERED THE
HAMMERING CON-
TEST.

Now arrange the circled letters to form the surprise answer, as suggested by the above cartoon.

Print answer here HE "  "

PUZZLE 47

Unscramble these four Jumbles, one letter to each square, to form four ordinary words.

TYPIE

REXET

TONPHY

RANTIM

One of my best customers

I'll take this too

WHAT SHE SPENT TO BUY NEW MAKEUP.

Now arrange the circled letters to form the surprise answer, as suggested by the above cartoon.

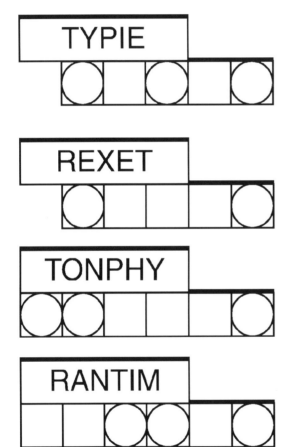

Print answer here A " ☐☐☐☐☐☐ " ☐☐☐☐☐

JUMBLE®

Unscramble these four Jumbles, one letter to each square, to form four ordinary words.

NOMUT

LAROF

CELLOA

CIANAM

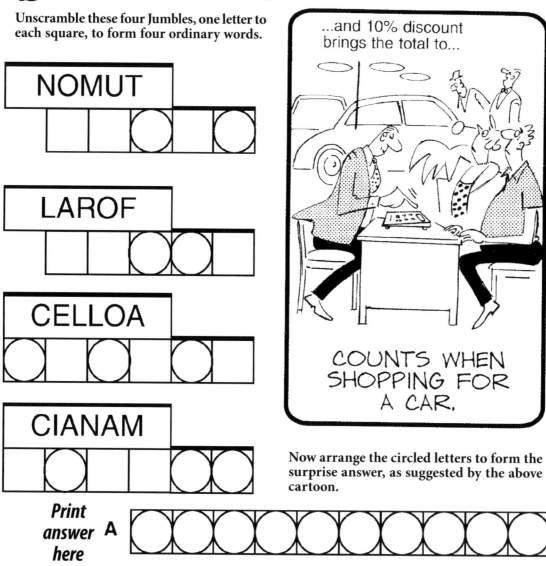

...and 10% discount brings the total to...

COUNTS WHEN SHOPPING FOR A CAR.

Now arrange the circled letters to form the surprise answer, as suggested by the above cartoon.

Print answer here **A**

50

JUMBLE®

Unscramble these four Jumbles, one letter to each square, to form four ordinary words.

WYLEN

JOANB

SWACHE

DIALIN

My last day...never saw the sun

THE MINER QUIT HIS JOB BECAUSE HE WAS---

Now arrange the circled letters to form the surprise answer, as suggested by the above cartoon.

Print answer here

"　"

JUMBLE®

Unscramble these four Jumbles, one letter to each square, to form four ordinary words.

TOANB

NOMEW

SEMQUO

BEJOCT

You didn't keep your
end of the bargain.
No car tonight

WHAT JUNIOR'S
PROMISE TURNED
OUT TO BE WHEN
THE DRIVEWAY
WASN'T CLEARED.

Now arrange the circled letters to form the surprise answer, as suggested by the above cartoon.

Print answer here A " ⃝⃝⃝⃝ " ⃝⃝⃝

JUMBLE

Unscramble these four Jumbles, one letter to each square, to form four ordinary words.

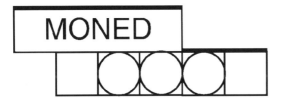

MONED

BOTOR

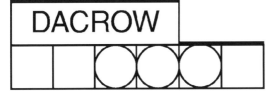

DACROW

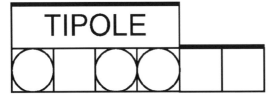

TIPOLE

Hey, where's my food? I'm starving

SUFFERED BY AN IMPATIENT DINER.

Now arrange the circled letters to form the surprise answer, as suggested by the above cartoon.

Print answer here A "⬡⬡⬡⬡" ⬡⬡⬡⬡⬡⬡⬡⬡

PUZZLE
52

JUMBLE®

Unscramble these four Jumbles, one letter to each square, to form four ordinary words.

YADIL

RYRUH

BOGTLE

NATIVY

I'm coming — Daddy's got your bottle

WAH WAH

WHAT THE JUDGE EXPERIENCED WHEN HE TOOK TIME OFF.

Now arrange the circled letters to form the surprise answer, as suggested by the above cartoon.

Print answer here A " ⬡⬡⬡⬡⬡⬡ " ⬡⬡⬡

54

PUZZLE 53

JUMBLE

Unscramble these four Jumbles, one letter to each square, to form four ordinary words.

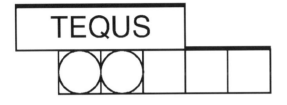

TEQUS

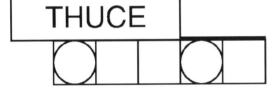

THUCE

GARCHE

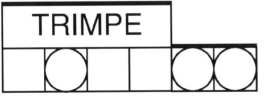

TRIMPE

She's gorgeous

Lucky guy

WHEN THE PLAYER MARRIED THE BEAUTY QUEEN IN CENTER FIELD, IT WAS----

Now arrange the circled letters to form the surprise answer, as suggested by the above cartoon.

Print answer here ⬡⬡⬡⬡⬡ A "⬡⬡⬡⬡⬡"

55

JUMBLE®

Unscramble these four Jumbles, one letter to each square, to form four ordinary words.

TUNYT

RAFIR

SHUBLE

DYNKIL

I got him in midair

THE CAMERAMAN CAPTURED THE WINNING BASKET---

Now arrange the circled letters to form the surprise answer, as suggested by the above cartoon.

Print answer here ◯◯ A " ◯◯◯◯◯ "

JUMBLE®

Unscramble these four Jumbles, one letter to each square, to form four ordinary words.

HACCO

NOMUD

DERAIV

LEEPPO

This time, I'm sure

IMPORTANT TO DO WHEN YOU MARRY TWICE.

Now arrange the circled letters to form the surprise answer, as suggested by the above cartoon.

Print answer here

JUMBLE®

Unscramble these four Jumbles, one letter to each square, to form four ordinary words.

UPYPP

TINJO

UNCLAY

MOABEA

I voted for you

How would you like some easy work?

WHAT THE POLI- TICIAN OFFERED THE POOR FRUIT PEDDLER.

Now arrange the circled letters to form the surprise answer, as suggested by the above cartoon.

Print answer here A "◯◯◯◯" ◯◯◯

JUMBLE®

Unscramble these four Jumbles, one letter to each square, to form four ordinary words.

MAIDT

KEREC

PENMAD

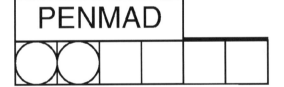

SCYTIK

You're in perfect health

Oh, yeah? I feel lousy

WHAT THE DOCTOR'S DIAGNOSIS DID TO THE HYPOCHONDRIAC.

Now arrange the circled letters to form the surprise answer, as suggested by the above cartoon.

Print answer here  HIM

JUMBLE

Unscramble these four Jumbles, one letter to each square, to form four ordinary words.

KANOE

DATUL

RETAIW

NEPELS

My divorce is final.
Let's get married

WHAT HE WANTED
TO DO WHEN HE
SETTLED UP
WITH HIS EX-
WIFE.

Now arrange the circled letters to form the surprise answer, as suggested by the above cartoon.

Print answer here

JUMBLE®

Unscramble these four Jumbles, one letter to each square, to form four ordinary words.

APITO

YASTT

ENGINS

REESHY

You'll simply have to do better, Hodgekiss

WHAT THE BOSS DID WHEN THE HIGHWAY STRIPER WASN'T CAREFUL.

Now arrange the circled letters to form the surprise answer, as suggested by the above cartoon.

Print answer here ☐☐☐ HIM "☐☐☐☐☐☐☐☐☐"

JUMBLE®

Unscramble these four Jumbles, one letter to each square, to form four ordinary words.

FOBEG

HYSYL

HASBIN

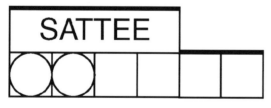

SATTEE

Notice the detail

They'll sell like hotcakes

WHEN THE LATEST STYLE SANDALS WERE INTRODUCED THEY WERE BOUND TO BE---

Now arrange the circled letters to form the surprise answer, as suggested by the above cartoon.

Print answer here A

PUZZLE 61

Unscramble these four Jumbles, one letter to each square, to form four ordinary words.

VENAK

CANKS

SNAZAT

PALLAP

We'll rest for an hour

WHAT SLEEPING BAGS CAN TURN INTO ON THE SPUR OF THE MOMENT.

Now arrange the circled letters to form the surprise answer, as suggested by the above cartoon.

Print answer here " ⃝⃝⃝ " ⃝⃝⃝⃝⃝

63

JUMBLE®

Unscramble these four Jumbles, one letter to each square, to form four ordinary words.

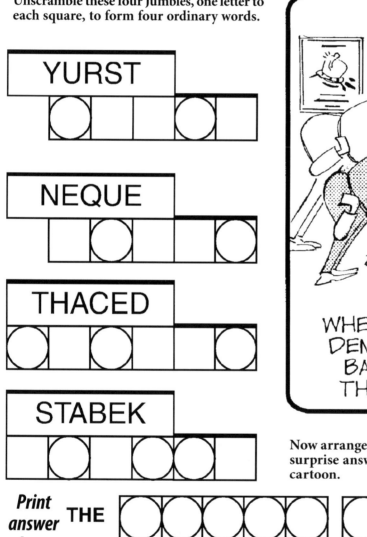

YURST

NEQUE

THACED

STABEK

Sure, I shot the dirty bum

WHEN THE COPS DEMANDED THE BARE FACTS, THEY GOT----

Now arrange the circled letters to form the surprise answer, as suggested by the above cartoon.

Print answer here **THE** ⬡⬡⬡⬡⬡⬡ ⬡⬡⬡⬡⬡⬡

JUMBLE.

Unscramble these four Jumbles, one letter to each square, to form four ordinary words.

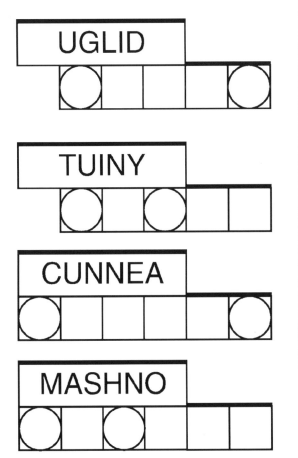

UGLID

TUINY

CUNNEA

MASHNO

HOW THE BUILDER REACTED WHEN THE DOOR WAS THE WRONG SIZE.

Now arrange the circled letters to form the surprise answer, as suggested by the above cartoon.

Print answer here HE GOT

JUMBLE®

Unscramble these four Jumbles, one letter to each square, to form four ordinary words.

IMPER

PINTE

YORPTS

ENMOAB

It's my
hobby

Lovely

WHAT SHE EARNED
BY SELLING HER
HANDMADE
BROOCHES.

Now arrange the circled letters to form the surprise answer, as suggested by the above cartoon.

Print answer here " ◯◯◯ " ◯◯◯◯◯◯

JUMBLE®

Unscramble these four Jumbles, one letter to each square, to form four ordinary words.

NIRPT

KREJY

DITNIC

DITNIC *(shown as DITNIC)*

DITNIC

TOAPIE

I told you no food or drinks in here

I'm cleaning it up

WHERE THE TEEN-AGER ENDED UP WHEN HE SPILLED THE DRINK.

Now arrange the circled letters to form the surprise answer, as suggested by the above cartoon.

Print answer here ⬡⬡ THE ⬡⬡⬡⬡⬡⬡

JUMBLE

Unscramble these four Jumbles, one letter to each square, to form four ordinary words.

MEFAD

RUGAU

CUPHIC

ROCCUN

How much did you spend?

Oh, just a trifle

A HUG FOR HUBBY AFTER A SHOPPING TRIP IS A GOOD WAY TO GET—

Now arrange the circled letters to form the surprise answer, as suggested by the above cartoon.

Print answer here "◯◯◯◯◯◯◯" ◯◯◯

68

JUMBLE®

Unscramble these four Jumbles, one letter to each square, to form four ordinary words.

MUGMY

YAIDS

MASTIG

ENGALB

WHAT THE SWITCH-
BOARD OPERATOR
GAVE HER BOSS.

Now arrange the circled letters to form the surprise answer, as suggested by the above cartoon.

Print answer here A " ⬡⬡⬡⬡ " ⬡⬡⬡⬡⬡⬡

JUMBLE®

Unscramble these four Jumbles, one letter to
each square, to form four ordinary words.

EDRIN

UTOOD

GATHIL

FRUGEE

WHO DID DRACULA
TAKE TO THE
HALLOWEEN PARTY?

Now arrange the circled letters to form the
surprise answer, as suggested by the above
cartoon.

Print
answer **A** " ◯◯◯◯◯ " ◯◯◯◯◯◯
here

JUMBLE®

Unscramble these four Jumbles, one letter to each square, to form four ordinary words.

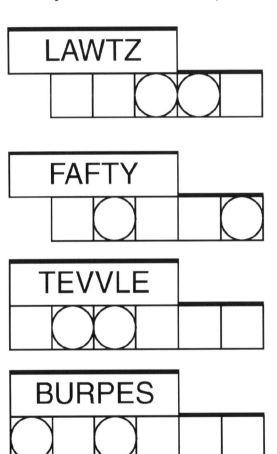

LAWTZ

FAFTY

TEVVLE

BURPES

ENCOUNTERED IN THE OLD PRINT SHOP.

Now arrange the circled letters to form the surprise answer, as suggested by the above cartoon.

Print answer here  " "

JUMBLE®

Unscramble these four Jumbles, one letter to each square, to form four ordinary words.

AKARP

VELIA

CAUABS

PENXED

He's their best hitter

THE JANITOR'S FAVORITE SPOT IN THE BATTING ORDER.

Now arrange the circled letters to form the surprise answer, as suggested by the above cartoon.

Print answer here

72

JUMBLE®

Unscramble these four Jumbles, one letter to each square, to form four ordinary words.

ROAHB

MYNEE

CYNAGE

VODURE

"#$%#!! Now I'm stranded

WHY THE SHIP-WRECKED SAILOR TURNED PURPLE WITH RAGE.

Now arrange the circled letters to form the surprise answer, as suggested by the above cartoon.

Print answer here HE WAS " ◯◯◯◯◯◯◯◯◯ "

JUMBLE®

Unscramble these four Jumbles, one letter to each square, to form four ordinary words.

VIRTE

RAFIE

GRAHAN

GOTTOR

I'm sure it's this one

NO! NO! NO!

THE GEOLOGY STUDENT FLUNKED HIS ROCKS EXAM BECAUSE HE TOOK——

Now arrange the circled letters to form the surprise answer, as suggested by the above cartoon.

Print answer IT here " "

JUMBLE®

Unscramble these four Jumbles, one letter to each square, to form four ordinary words.

HELEW

LAGED

GYFFIE

SNIDUM

He's so handsome   ...and fast!

WHY THEY WERE ATTRACTED TO THE SPRINTER.

Now arrange the circled letters to form the surprise answer, as suggested by the above cartoon.

Print answer here   **HE WAS**   "◯◯◯◯◯◯◯"

JUMBLE®

Unscramble these four Jumbles, one letter to each square, to form four ordinary words.

POSOT

SCUHR

FRUTOH

VEEDIC

Phew! That could have been ME!

WHEN HE TOOK HIS EX-GIRL'S BRIDAL PHOTOS, HE WAS----

Now arrange the circled letters to form the surprise answer, as suggested by the above cartoon.

Print answer here

[⃝⃝⃝] OF THE [⃝⃝⃝⃝⃝⃝⃝]

JUMBLE

Unscramble these four Jumbles, one letter to
each square, to form four ordinary words.

ALCAN

INLOG

BAMGEL

SAUCCU

Never a free
minute

HOW THE FOOD
CRITIC DESCRIBED
HIS JOB.

Now arrange the circled letters to form the
surprise answer, as suggested by the above
cartoon.

Print
answer
here

" "

JUMBLE®

Unscramble these four Jumbles, one letter to each square, to form four ordinary words.

NICEW

RUHTT

ENPOTT

INLOVI

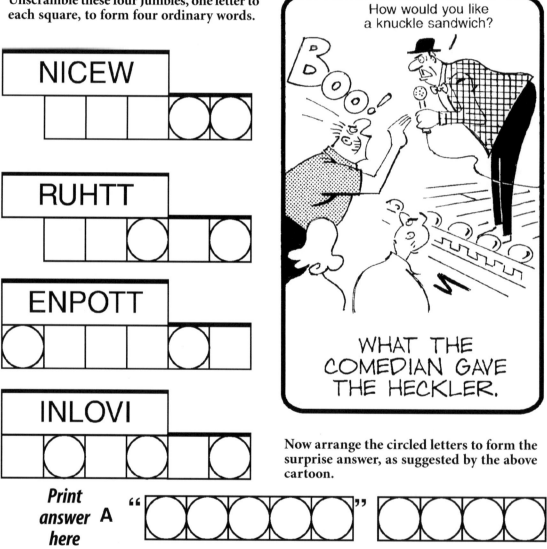

How would you like a knuckle sandwich?

BOO!

WHAT THE COMEDIAN GAVE THE HECKLER.

Now arrange the circled letters to form the surprise answer, as suggested by the above cartoon.

Print answer here A " ⬡⬡⬡⬡⬡ " ⬡⬡⬡⬡

JUMBLE.

Unscramble these four Jumbles, one letter to each square, to form four ordinary words.

MIFLY

GANYM

FORPIT

VAQUER

I need this to look decent

WHAT SHE KEPT IN HER MAKEUP CASE.

Now arrange the circled letters to form the surprise answer, as suggested by the above cartoon.

Print answer here " ◯◯◯◯◯◯ " ◯◯◯◯

JUMBLE®

Unscramble these four Jumbles, one letter to each square, to form four ordinary words.

ORPYX

OMBOL

JORNAG

SUMOFA

In six months I'll be in the big time

DEVELOPED BY THE GIFTED MINOR-LEAGUE PLAYER.

Now arrange the circled letters to form the surprise answer, as suggested by the above cartoon.

Print answer here " ⬡⬡⬡⬡⬡ " ⬡⬡⬡⬡⬡

Unscramble these four Jumbles, one letter to
each square, to form four ordinary words.

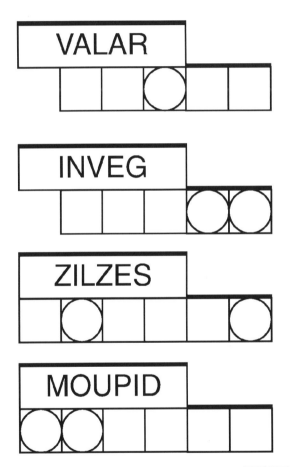

VALAR

INVEG

ZILZES

MOUPID

The name of this handsome
guy standing before
you is Bill

WHAT SHE CON-
SIDERED HIS
INTRODUCTION AT
THE SINGLES
BAR.

Now arrange the circled letters to form the
surprise answer, as suggested by the above
cartoon.

Print answer here AN " ⬡ " ⬡⬡⬡⬡⬡⬡

JUMBLE®

Unscramble these four Jumbles, one letter to each square, to form four ordinary words.

SECAE

FIBTE

GLANID

TIFONY

Mommy loves her itsy-bitsy cute-ums

WHEN THE TABBY CUDDLED ON HER LAP, SHE WAS----

Now arrange the circled letters to form the surprise answer, as suggested by the above cartoon.

Print answer here " ⟳⟳⟳⟳⟳⟳ " ⟳⟳⟳⟳

JUMBLE®

Unscramble these four Jumbles, one letter to
each square, to form four ordinary words.

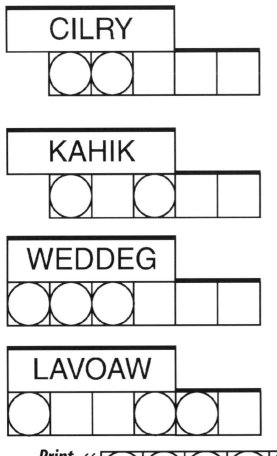

CILRY

KAHIK

WEDDEG

LAVOAW

Three free passes in —
a row. Bases loaded

WZBT

Take a
shower

WHAT THE PITCHER
DID WHEN HE
COULDN'T THROW
A STRIKE.

Now arrange the circled letters to form the
surprise answer, as suggested by the above
cartoon.

Print "
answer
here
"

83

JUMBLE®

Unscramble these four Jumbles, one letter to each square, to form four ordinary words.

TELIT

ROWBE

TARIBB

YAUBET

First, pay attention to the dealer's face card, then...

HE TOOK BLACK-JACK LESSONS TO BECOME---

Now arrange the circled letters to form the surprise answer, as suggested by the above cartoon.

Print answer here   A

JUMBLE

Unscramble these four Jumbles, one letter to
each square, to form four ordinary words.

GARBE

LULET

RITHEM

NACTAV

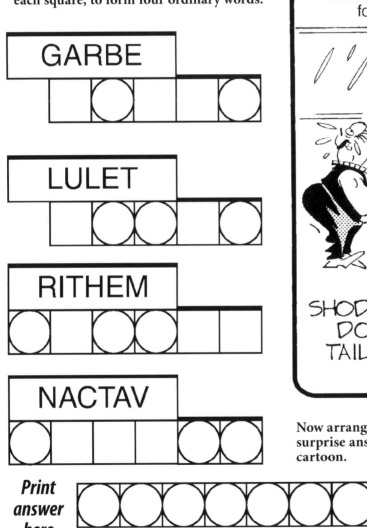

I'm not paying
for this

SHODDY WORK WILL
DO THIS TO A
TAILOR'S SALES.

Now arrange the circled letters to form the
surprise answer, as suggested by the above
cartoon.

**Print
answer
here**

85

Unscramble these four Jumbles, one letter to
each square, to form four ordinary words.

NAPAG

WIHSS

CILTIE

DINBAT

I get the
house and
the car

No, I get
the...

Get me an
aspirin

THE KIND OF
HEADACHE A
DIVORCE CAN
CAUSE.

Now arrange the circled letters to form the
surprise answer, as suggested by the above
cartoon.

Print answer here " ◯◯◯◯◯◯◯◯◯ "

JUMBLE®

Unscramble these four Jumbles, one letter to each square, to form four ordinary words.

LAVIT

LAANB

LESUNS

YARWIA

It's getting worn out

Perhaps a brighter color

WHY SHE SOUGHT NEW FABRIC FOR THE WELL-USED EASY CHAIR.

Now arrange the circled letters to form the surprise answer, as suggested by the above cartoon.

Print answer here IT ◯◯◯ "◯◯◯-◯◯"

JUMBLE®

Unscramble these four Jumbles, one letter to each square, to form four ordinary words.

RAICH

TAMEL

FREIHE

WEFURC

I hope it doesn't rain

WHAT THE TOWN HOPED FOR DURING THE ANNUAL CAR-NIVAL DAYS.

Now arrange the circled letters to form the surprise answer, as suggested by the above cartoon.

Print answer here

JUMBLE

Unscramble these four Jumbles, one letter to
each square, to form four ordinary words.

WOSOP

EPSIO

TOXICE

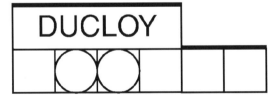

DUCLOY

These seedlings
need sun
and water

IMPORTANT FOR A
ROOF GARDEN.

Now arrange the circled letters to form the
surprise answer, as suggested by the above
cartoon.

Print answer here "  "

JUMBLE.

Unscramble these four Jumbles, one letter to each square, to form four ordinary words.

RAVSO

DEWUN

KONYED

REVUIQ

Shut them up!

I'm calling the cops

Polly wants a cracker!

Awk!

WHAT THE NEIGH-
BORS DID ABOUT
THE NOISY
PARROTS.

Now arrange the circled letters to form the surprise answer, as suggested by the above cartoon.

Print answer here " ◯◯◯◯◯◯◯◯◯ "

JUMBLE®

Unscramble these four Jumbles, one letter to each square, to form four ordinary words.

TOABB

TEELI

PLIDIM

NERRED

He's got the talent and desire

78

HE BECAME A CHAMPION RACER BY PUTTING HIS----

Now arrange the circled letters to form the surprise answer, as suggested by the above cartoon.

Print answer here " ◯◯◯◯◯◯◯ " TO THE ◯◯◯◯◯

91

PUZZLE
90

JUMBLE

Unscramble these four Jumbles, one letter to each square, to form four ordinary words.

SYRTT

CUROC

KOVINE

REPUPA

WHEN THE BOATERS LANDED IN THE MIDDLE OF THE LAKE, THEY WERE———

Now arrange the circled letters to form the surprise answer, as suggested by the above cartoon.

Print answer here

92

JUMBLE®

Unscramble these four Jumbles, one letter to each square, to form four ordinary words.

SELBS

DRUFA

FIMSIT

DEBISE

Phew! Not me!

No, thanks

THE TURKEY AND THE FAMILY WERE THIS ON THANKSGIVING.

Now arrange the circled letters to form the surprise answer, as suggested by the above cartoon.

Print answer here "⬤⬤⬤⬤⬤⬤⬤"

93

JUMBLE®

Unscramble these four Jumbles, one letter to each square, to form four ordinary words.

LEEBI

MOBIL

NETTAX

NORZEF

Hey, I didn't order meat!

WHEN THE VEGE-TARIAN YELLED AT THE SERVER, HE HAD A ---

Now arrange the circled letters to form the surprise answer, as suggested by the above cartoon.

Print answer here

JUMBLE®

Unscramble these four Jumbles, one letter to
each square, to form four ordinary words.

ARREM

DARRO

WHYANO

DAVULE

I'm getting tarred up
here. Get it? Har har!

THE HELPER
DIDN'T LAUGH AT
THE ROOFER'S
JOKE BECAUSE
IT WAS----

Now arrange the circled letters to form the
surprise answer, as suggested by the above
cartoon.

Print answer here ◯◯◯◯ **HIS** ◯◯◯◯

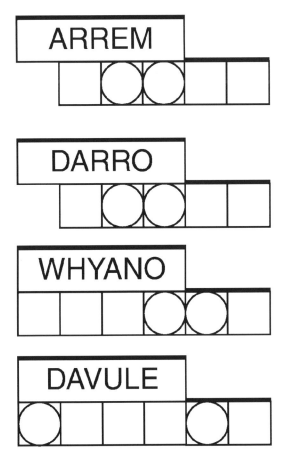

JUMBLE®

Unscramble these four Jumbles, one letter to each square, to form four ordinary words.

BYRIN

SEGIN

PICOMY

NIGMIT

I'll call you tomorrow for sure

SHE GAVE HIM A GOOD-NIGHT KISS BECAUSE HE SEEMED----

Now arrange the circled letters to form the surprise answer, as suggested by the above cartoon.

Print answer here " ◯◯◯◯◯◯◯◯◯ "

JUMBLE

Unscramble these four Jumbles, one letter to each square, to form four ordinary words.

THECK

RACCK

SAKMAD

CARNID

I can't believe I lost again

Aw, quit your moaning

HARDER TO DEAL WITH AFTER A WHILE.

Now arrange the circled letters to form the surprise answer, as suggested by the above cartoon.

Print answer here

A ◯◯◯◯ OF ◯◯◯◯◯

97

JUMBLE®

Unscramble these four Jumbles, one letter to each square, to form four ordinary words.

WHEGI

YEMSS

TIPIDE

TARNEK

AFTER EATING ALL THAT CHOCOLATE, JUNIOR FELL ASLEEP AND HAD----

Now arrange the circled letters to form the surprise answer, as suggested by the above cartoon.

Print answer here " _____ " _____

JUMBLE®

Unscramble these four Jumbles, one letter to each square, to form four ordinary words.

WYDON

YOOST

DAGOIA

ROOLIE

Make sure you close your *O*s

a b c d e f g h i j k

STRESSED IN A PENMANSHIP CLASS.

Now arrange the circled letters to form the surprise answer, as suggested by the above cartoon.

Print answer here ⬚⬚⬚⬚⬚ IT " ⬚⬚⬚⬚⬚ "

JUMBLE®

Unscramble these four Jumbles, one letter to each square, to form four ordinary words.

GHEED

GLITH

TRUIPY

LEEMOT

Throw him in the slammer

WHAT THE JUDGE DID TO THE PHONE THIEF.

Now arrange the circled letters to form the surprise answer, as suggested by the above cartoon.

Print answer here ⬛⬛⬛ ⬛⬛⬛ ON "⬛⬛⬛⬛"

JUMBLE®

Unscramble these four Jumbles, one letter to each square, to form four ordinary words.

SEGUS

CANTE

HAWRTT

RIMBAU

Got one

SWACK!

Me, too

WHAT THE PIC-NICKERS FORMED TO BATTLE THE INSECTS.

Now arrange the circled letters to form the surprise answer, as suggested by the above cartoon.

Print answer here A " ⬡⬡⬡⬡ " ⬡⬡⬡⬡

JUMBLE

Unscramble these four Jumbles, one letter to each square, to form four ordinary words.

GLIVI

LAIGE

GLIEGG

SMIFAH

...ha ha. Get it?

I've heard that one 10 times

WHEN HE KEPT REPEATING THE OLD JOKES, THE HOST WANTED TO——

Now arrange the circled letters to form the surprise answer, as suggested by the above cartoon.

Print answer here ⬡⬡⬡⬡ ⬡⬡⬡ A "⬡⬡⬡"

JUMBLE®

Unscramble these four Jumbles, one letter to each square, to form four ordinary words.

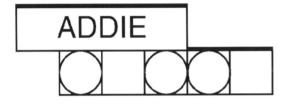

ADDIE

OXTIN

BOWELL

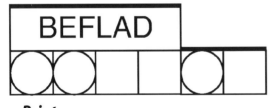

BEFLAD

George always was antisocial

WHAT THE BANKER DID.

Now arrange the circled letters to form the surprise answer, as suggested by the above cartoon.

Print answer here

"   "

JUMBLE®

Unscramble these four Jumbles, one letter to each square, to form four ordinary words.

GUNDE

CITOX

STUJYL

ETTIPE

It's a bit pricey. We'll let you know tomorrow

$1500

WHAT THE COUPLE DID WHEN THEY COULDN'T DECIDE ON A MATTRESS.

Now arrange the circled letters to form the surprise answer, as suggested by the above cartoon.

Print answer here " ⬭⬭⬭⬭⬭ " ⬭⬭ ⬭⬭

JUMBLE®

Unscramble these four Jumbles, one letter to each square, to form four ordinary words.

REPPA

KLEAN

LANGAR

BRYCAB

Oh, that's much too revealing

SHE DIDN'T BUY THE BIKINI BECAUSE SHE COULDN'T---

Now arrange the circled letters to form the surprise answer, as suggested by the above cartoon.

Print answer here ⬡⬡⬡⬡ TO ⬡⬡⬡⬡

JUMBLE®

Unscramble these four Jumbles, one letter to
each square, to form four ordinary words.

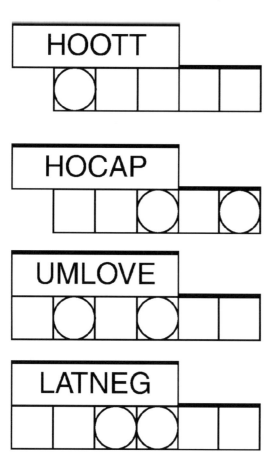

HOOTT

HOCAP

UMLOVE

LATNEG

Ah, this
is the
life

A HAMMOCK IS
A GOOD PLACE
TO DO THIS ON
A SUMMER DAY.

Now arrange the circled letters to form the
surprise answer, as suggested by the above
cartoon.

Print answer here " ◯◯◯◯ " ◯◯◯

JUMBLE®

Unscramble these four Jumbles, one letter to each square, to form four ordinary words.

INGYL

GUBYL

VOGNER

MOINCE

He's really good at this

I'll check my E-mail

THE LUMBERJACK'S FAVORITE TASK ON A COMPUTER.

Now arrange the circled letters to form the surprise answer, as suggested by the above cartoon.

Print answer here "◯◯◯◯◯◯◯" ◯◯

JUMBLE®

Unscramble these four Jumbles, one letter to
each square, to form four ordinary words.

ODITI

PITED

GRYPIN

WETING

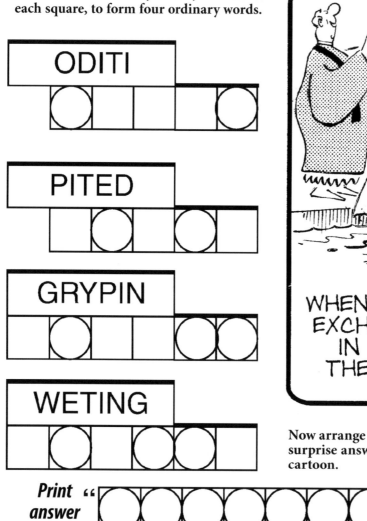

Do you, Tom,
take---

WHEN THE COUPLE
EXCHANGED VOWS
IN THE POOL,
THEY WERE ----

Now arrange the circled letters to form the
surprise answer, as suggested by the above
cartoon.

Print   "◯◯◯◯◯◯◯"   ◯◯◯
answer
here

JUMBLE®

Unscramble these four Jumbles, one letter to each square, to form four ordinary words.

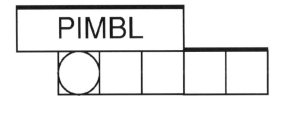

PIMBL

DUJEG

YALAWY

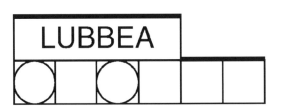

LUBBEA

My credit cards are maxed out

WHAT SHE SAID WHEN SHE QUIT SHOPPING TO SAVE MONEY.

Now arrange the circled letters to form the surprise answer, as suggested by the above cartoon.

Print answer here

JUMBLE

Unscramble these four Jumbles, one letter to each square, to form four ordinary words.

ILLAC

SOBAS

TAUROH

FHABLE

My feet are killing me

WHY THE SHY WIFE WANTED TO GO HOME FROM THE PARTY.

Now arrange the circled letters to form the surprise answer, as suggested by the above cartoon.

Print answer here   SHE WAS " ◯◯◯◯ " ◯◯◯◯

JUMBLE®

Unscramble these four Jumbles, one letter to each square, to form four ordinary words.

GYDUP

TASUE

CARFIB

HEWZEE

He's not really important around here

WHAT THE CHIEF OF THE ACCOUNT-ING STAFF WAS KNOWN AS.

Now arrange the circled letters to form the surprise answer, as suggested by the above cartoon.

Print answer here

A " ☐◯☐◯☐◯☐◯☐◯☐◯ " ☐◯☐◯☐◯

JUMBLE®

Unscramble these four Jumbles, one letter to each square, to form four ordinary words.

DRATY

MUBIE

LATMEL

SHRUPE

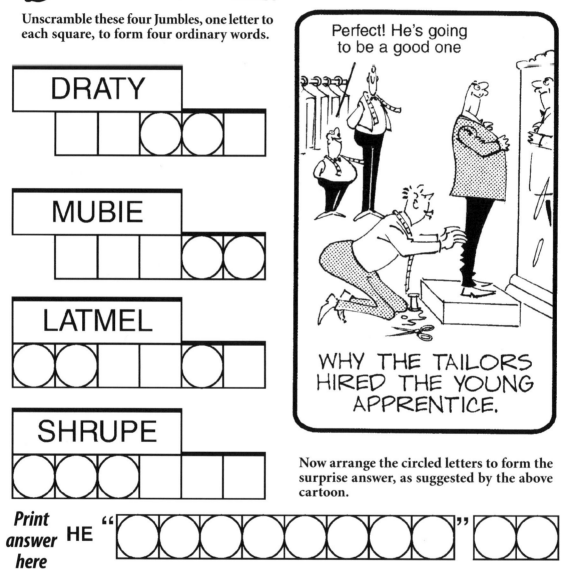

Perfect! He's going to be a good one

WHY THE TAILORS HIRED THE YOUNG APPRENTICE.

Now arrange the circled letters to form the surprise answer, as suggested by the above cartoon.

Print answer here HE "〇〇〇〇〇〇〇〇〇" 〇〇

JUMBLE®

Unscramble these four Jumbles, one letter to each square, to form four ordinary words.

BOGUM

GORAC

ZELPUZ

STERJE

Let's get married, J.B.

WHAT THE RIVAL EXECUTIVES DISCUSSED WHEN THEY FELL IN LOVE.

Now arrange the circled letters to form the surprise answer, as suggested by the above cartoon.

Print answer here THE ◯◯◯◯◯ TO ◯◯◯◯◯◯

JUMBLE.

Unscramble these four Jumbles, one letter to each square, to form four ordinary words.

RILLT

KOYLE

SNIPOO

ENWAKE

LOVE IS FOR THE YOUNG

THESE HEADLINES CAN UPSET AN AGING FASHION EDITOR.

Now arrange the circled letters to form the surprise answer, as suggested by the above cartoon.

Print answer here

114

JUMBLE.

Unscramble these four Jumbles, one letter to each square, to form four ordinary words.

TACHY

ROBIT

INSECK

SINVIO

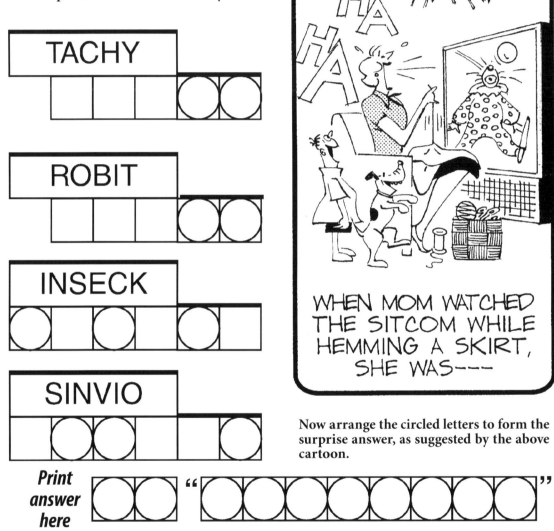

WHEN MOM WATCHED THE SITCOM WHILE HEMMING A SKIRT, SHE WAS----

Now arrange the circled letters to form the surprise answer, as suggested by the above cartoon.

Print answer here

⬡⬡ " ⬡⬡⬡⬡⬡⬡⬡⬡ "

JUMBLE®

Unscramble these four Jumbles, one letter to each square, to form four ordinary words.

ESROU

WEDIP

CYTHAC

FICTEN

The perfume here is cheap

Nothing but fun and games

WHAT THE SAILORS LIKED BEST DURING THEIR LEAVE OVERSEAS.

Now arrange the circled letters to form the surprise answer, as suggested by the above cartoon.

Print answer here IT WAS " ◯◯◯◯ " ◯◯◯◯

JUMBLE®

Unscramble these four Jumbles, one letter to each square, to form four ordinary words.

KYDUS

HOBUG

NOALOS

DILBOE

Nobody will suspect me

WHY THE BEAUTY QUEEN BECAME A SPY.

Now arrange the circled letters to form the surprise answer, as suggested by the above cartoon.

Print answer here

SHE "◯◯◯◯◯◯" ◯◯◯◯

JUMBLE®

Unscramble these four Jumbles, one letter to each square, to form four ordinary words.

OINES

ROFEY

FULOWE

TREFFO

Gotcha

THE COPS CAUGHT THE PICKPOCKET WITH QUICK HANDS BECAUSE OF THIS.

Now arrange the circled letters to form the surprise answer, as suggested by the above cartoon.

Print answer here

JUMBLE

Unscramble these four Jumbles, one letter to each square, to form four ordinary words.

NASDY

DRYBE

THUBOG

NATTIC

Just a few quick puffs and it's back to work

PUFF

PUFF

PUFF

WHAT THE OFFICE WORKER SAID WHEN HE RUSHED OUTSIDE FOR A SMOKE.

Now arrange the circled letters to form the surprise answer, as suggested by the above cartoon.

Print answer here ◯◯'◯ A "◯◯◯◯"

JUMBLE®

Unscramble these four Jumbles, one letter to each square, to form four ordinary words.

NIYKK

BLAYM

NOJINE

BIEMIB

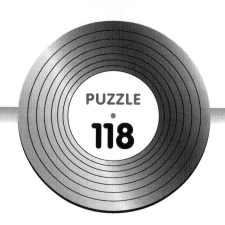

You have the most gorgeous eyes

A QUARTERBACK CAN TURN INTO THIS ON THE BENCH.

Now arrange the circled letters to form the surprise answer, as suggested by the above cartoon.

Print answer here A " ◯◯◯◯ " ◯◯◯

JUMBLE®

Unscramble these four Jumbles, one letter to each square, to form four ordinary words.

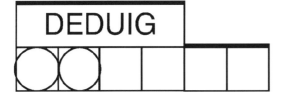

HUDCY

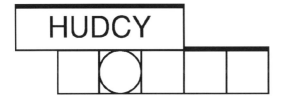

FYLOT

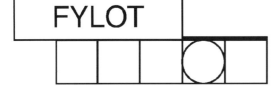

DEDUIG

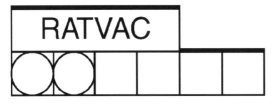

RATVAC

It feels like we're on a cloud

WHAT THE COUPLE DID WHEN THE CARPETING WAS INSTALLED.

Now arrange the circled letters to form the surprise answer, as suggested by the above cartoon.

Print answer here

 A

JUMBLE.

Unscramble these four Jumbles, one letter to each square, to form four ordinary words.

ZACER

PHEES

QUIROL

VIPSEL

They give me more traction

THE UPHOLSTERER SAID THE CHAINS ON HIS TIRES WERE----

Now arrange the circled letters to form the surprise answer, as suggested by the above cartoon.

Print answer here " ◯◯◯◯ " ◯◯◯◯◯◯◯

JUMBLE®

Unscramble these four Jumbles, one letter to each square, to form four ordinary words.

THICH

IRATT

IMBAGT

GOTFER

WHAT THE BARFLIES RESORTED TO WHEN THEY HAD AN ARGUMENT.

Now arrange the circled letters to form the surprise answer, as suggested by the above cartoon.

Print answer here   A "◯◯◯◯◯" ◯◯◯◯◯◯

123

JUMBLE®

Unscramble these four Jumbles, one letter to each square, to form four ordinary words.

PIERG

LOCON

YIPRAC

FADGYL

Just $10,000

THIS CAN BE HARDER THAN A DIAMOND.

Now arrange the circled letters to form the surprise answer, as suggested by the above cartoon.

Print answer here ⬡⬡⬡⬡⬡⬡⬡ ⬡⬡⬡ IT

JUMBLE®

Unscramble these four Jumbles, one letter to
each square, to form four ordinary words.

RASCY

UGIED

NARCLE

NAHMLY

Let's go to
Le Snob
tonight

Nobody
would
recognize
you

WHAT THE CLOWN
LOOKED LIKE WHEN
HE DRESSED FOR
HIS BIG DATE.

Now arrange the circled letters to form the
surprise answer, as suggested by the above
cartoon.

*Print
answer
here*   A   " ◯◯◯◯◯◯◯ " ◯◯◯

JUMBLE

Unscramble these four Jumbles, one letter to each square, to form four ordinary words.

YETID
◯◯◯◯◯

WOPER
◯◯◯◯◯

GLOIBE
◯◯◯◯◯◯

RUTTEL
◯◯◯◯◯◯

made 30 calls in five hours

HOW THE NAPKIN SALESMAN FELT AT THE END OF THE DAY.

Now arrange the circled letters to form the surprise answer, as suggested by the above cartoon.

Print answer here " ◯◯◯◯◯ " ◯◯◯

JUMBLE

Unscramble these four Jumbles, one letter to each square, to form four ordinary words.

SCOUF

LALIV

STYLUB

CHOPON

The meat will cost about $50 a pound

I've got him

WHAT IT CAN COST TO GO AFTER BIG BUCKS.

Now arrange the circled letters to form the surprise answer, as suggested by the above cartoon.

Print answer here ◯◯◯◯ OF ◯◯◯◯

JUMBLE®

Unscramble these four Jumbles, one letter to each square, to form four ordinary words.

FREEW

NARVE

NABACA

DIAMER

First prize

HIS FAMILY LOOKED ON PROUDLY BECAUSE THE BAKER WAS THEIR----

Now arrange the circled letters to form the surprise answer, as suggested by the above cartoon.

Print answer here "⬭⬭⬭⬭⬭⬭⬭⬭⬭⬭⬭"

JUMBLE®

Unscramble these four Jumbles, one letter to
each square, to form four ordinary words.

REMEG

YORAF

AMLAMM

DRATOW

"Are you sure you've got the dates right? How is the food? Is it an outside cabin? Do we get snacks? Is it..."

Have a nice trip

WHAT THE TRAVEL AGENT WANTED THE PESKY CUSTOMER TO DO.

Now arrange the circled letters to form the
surprise answer, as suggested by the above
cartoon.

Print answer here

JUMBLE®

Unscramble these four Jumbles, one letter to each square, to form four ordinary words.

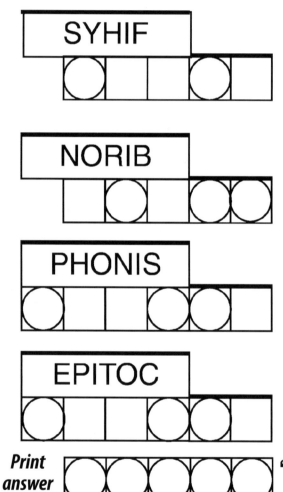

SYHIF

NORIB

PHONIS

EPITOC

This is suitable for framing

WHEN HE DEVEL-
OPED THE PORTRAIT
OF THE RACEHORSE,
IT WAS A----

Now arrange the circled letters to form the surprise answer, as suggested by the above cartoon.

Print answer here

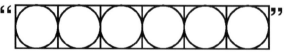

" "

JUMBLE®

Unscramble these four Jumbles, one letter to each square, to form four ordinary words.

RANGL

HILTE

CLOSIA

CRADOC

ACHOO!!

Hey, I don't want your cold

HE BECAME A FISHERMAN BECAUSE IT WAS----

Now arrange the circled letters to form the surprise answer, as suggested by the above cartoon.

Print answer here " ◯◯◯◯◯◯◯◯ "

131

JUMBLE®

Unscramble these four Jumbles, one letter to each square, to form four ordinary words.

INHEW

BAFLE

GITHEY

GLENET

Horace, I'm afraid you will never be successful in this line of work. Beat it!

THE DRAPERY HELPER WAS FIRED BECAUSE HE COULDN'T---

Now arrange the circled letters to form the surprise answer, as suggested by the above cartoon.

Print answer here

"⬡⬡⬡⬡" OF IT

JUMBLE®

Unscramble these four Jumbles, one letter to
each square, to form four ordinary words.

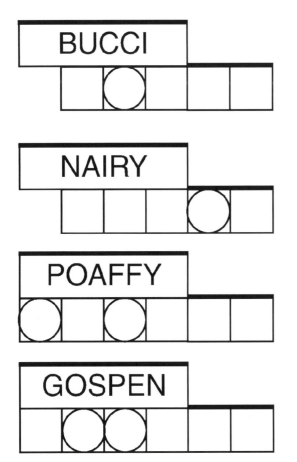

BUCCI

NAIRY

POAFFY

GOSPEN

You lose! Ten bucks, please

WHAT A BETTOR
HAS TO DO WHEN
HIS HORSE
LOSES THE RACE.

Now arrange the circled letters to form the
surprise answer, as suggested by the above
cartoon.

Print answer here

JUMBLE®

Unscramble these four Jumbles, one letter to each square, to form four ordinary words.

NADDY

ORRAM

JOUFLY

GLEFUN

We award the defendant $1,000

Aren't they super?

WHEN HE WAS ACQUITTED, THE DEFENDANT SAID HE HAD ---

Now arrange the circled letters to form the surprise answer, as suggested by the above cartoon.

Print answer here   A   " ⬡⬡⬡⬡⬡ " ⬡⬡⬡⬡

JUMBLE®

Unscramble these four Jumbles, one letter to each square, to form four ordinary words.

CENEF

UNHAM

UNGATH

PERMUB

Is this right?

A NOVICE GAR-
DENER IS SURE
TO HAVE THIS.

Now arrange the circled letters to form the surprise answer, as suggested by the above cartoon.

Print answer here   A " ◯◯◯◯◯ " ◯◯◯◯◯

JUMBLE®

Unscramble these four Jumbles, one letter to
each square, to form four ordinary words.

FEWAR

YUSUR

CYGERL

Good!
That'll
hold 'em
for a while

WHAT THE SHIP'S
BARBER GAVE THE
SAILORS.

STYMIC

Now arrange the circled letters to form the
surprise answer, as suggested by the above
cartoon.

Print answer here " ◯◯◯◯ " ◯◯◯◯

JUMBLE®

Unscramble these four Jumbles, one letter to each square, to form four ordinary words.

MUPLE

IRYAH

PANKID

VOMITE

Sunny all day, folks!

RAIN CAN DO THIS TO PICNIC PLANS.

Now arrange the circled letters to form the surprise answer, as suggested by the above cartoon.

Print answer here "◯◯◯◯◯◯◯" ◯◯◯◯

137

PUZZLE 136

JUMBLE

Unscramble these four Jumbles, one letter to each square, to form four ordinary words.

TOXEL

MOACE

INDIGH

YEAWLE

I'm not giving up

Let's go upstream

WHEN THE TROUT WEREN'T BITING, THE FISHERMEN HAD TO----

Now arrange the circled letters to form the surprise answer, as suggested by the above cartoon.

Print answer here " ⃝⃝⃝⃝⃝ " FOR ⃝⃝⃝⃝

138

JUMBLE®

Unscramble these four Jumbles, one letter to each square, to form four ordinary words.

LUGYL

HOLEL

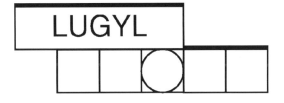

BROJEB

DUBBEG

Two feet, three inches. Mark that down

Yes, your majesty

WHAT THE KING DID WHEN THE CASTLE WAS REMODELED.

Now arrange the circled letters to form the surprise answer, as suggested by the above cartoon.

Print answer here ⬜⬜ " ⬜⬜⬜⬜⬜ "

JUMBLE

Unscramble these four Jumbles, one letter to each square, to form four ordinary words.

TAFUL

RAPAT

CUSCOT

YORPOL

Nice game

Er...about that traffic ticket, your honor...

WHY THE TENNIS CHAMP PLAYED A MATCH WITH THE JUDGE.

Now arrange the circled letters to form the surprise answer, as suggested by the above cartoon.

Print answer here

TO ⬡⬡⬡⬡⬡ THE ⬡⬡⬡⬡⬡

JUMBLE®

Unscramble these four Jumbles, one letter to each square, to form four ordinary words.

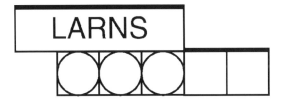

LARNS

PRUET

MNADAM

GREJIG

I can get close up with this lens

WHAT A PHOTO-GRAPHER NEEDS WHEN SHOOTING A SPORTS EVENT.

Now arrange the circled letters to form the surprise answer, as suggested by the above cartoon.

Print answer here " ⬡⬡⬡⬡⬡ " ⬡⬡⬡⬡⬡⬡⬡⬡⬡

JUMBLE®

Unscramble these four Jumbles, one letter to each square, to form four ordinary words.

LINTE

SAYGS

URIADS

SLUDOH

Nothing comes out right

Do we have anything for an upset stomach?

SHE THREW AWAY THE COOKBOOK BECAUSE IT WAS----

Now arrange the circled letters to form the surprise answer, as suggested by the above cartoon.

Print answer here

⟨◯◯◯◯⟩ TO "◯◯◯◯◯◯"

JUMBLE®

Unscramble these four Jumbles, one letter to each square, to form four ordinary words.

IGSEE

CHUGO

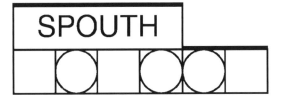
SPOUTH

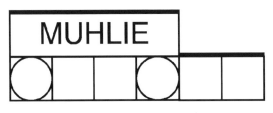
MUHLIE

You can do it, Rodney

Gosh, coach, 25 feet...I wonder...

WHAT THE POLE VAULTER HAD BEFORE THE COMPETITION.

Now arrange the circled letters to form the surprise answer, as suggested by the above cartoon.

Print answer here " ⬡⬡⬡⬡ " ⬡⬡⬡⬡⬡

JUMBLE®

Unscramble these four Jumbles, one letter to
each square, to form four ordinary words.

TULGI

ABOOT

REMMOY

DEBIHN

First it's football,
then baseball, then
soccer, then...

WHAT THE ZOO-
KEEPER TURNED INTO
EVERY WEEKEND.

Now arrange the circled letters to form the
surprise answer, as suggested by the above
cartoon.

*Print
answer* A
here
" ⬡⬡⬡⬡ " ⬡⬡⬡⬡⬡⬡

144

JUMBLE®

Unscramble these four Jumbles, one letter to each square, to form four ordinary words.

AHTEB

KAWTE

SNORGT

GRINTY

Who'll notice?

WHEN SHE BOUGHT HER CRUISE WEAR, SHE MADE SURE IT WAS---

Now arrange the circled letters to form the surprise answer, as suggested by the above cartoon.

Print answer here " ◯◯◯ " ◯◯◯◯◯◯◯

JUMBLE®

Unscramble these four Jumbles, one letter to each square, to form four ordinary words.

TEGOB

TRYAR

FLUINS

YURLOH

And the book-of-the-year award is presented to his majesty

The rich get richer

He'll make a pretty penny

WHAT THE KING RECEIVED FOR HIS AUTOBIOGRAPHY.

Now arrange the circled letters to form the surprise answer, as suggested by the above cartoon.

Print answer here " ⬡⬡⬡⬡⬡ – ⬡⬡⬡⬡ "

JUMBLE

Unscramble these four Jumbles, one letter to
each square, to form four ordinary words.

CREMY

THIRM

CUTLED

LAXAGY

Turn
down
that
noise

HOW GRANDPA FELT
WHEN THE KIDS
LISTENED TO
RAP MUSIC.

Now arrange the circled letters to form the
surprise answer, as suggested by the above
cartoon.

Print answer here "◯◯◯ – ◯◯◯◯◯◯"

JUMBLE®

Unscramble these four Jumbles, one letter to each square, to form four ordinary words.

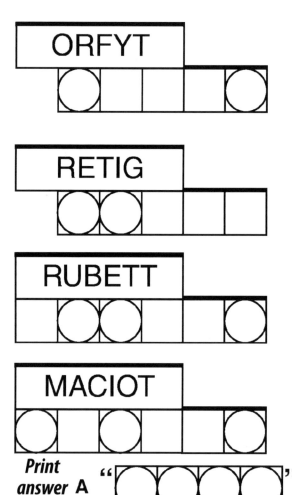

ORFYT

RETIG

RUBETT

MACIOT

WHAT THE BEAUTY QUEEN WORE WHEN SHE GREETED THE WINNING DRIVER.

Now arrange the circled letters to form the surprise answer, as suggested by the above cartoon.

Print answer A here " "

148

JUMBLE®

Unscramble these four Jumbles, one letter to each square, to form four ordinary words.

BOVAR

YICIL

RELOAP

CHEELK

Your final grade

How'd you do?

So so

WHERE THE STUDENT ENDED UP WHEN HE COMPLETED THE SAILING COURSE.

Now arrange the circled letters to form the surprise answer, as suggested by the above cartoon.

Print answer here   AT " ☐ " ☐☐☐☐☐☐

JUMBLE®

Unscramble these four Jumbles, one letter to each square, to form four ordinary words.

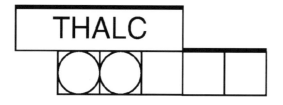

THALC

KEHRI

NAITLE

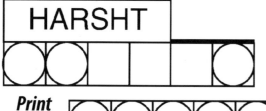

HARSHT

I've had too many

I feel woozy myself

THE BARFLIES GOT SICK BECAUSE THEY IMBIBED TOO OFTEN TO----

Now arrange the circled letters to form the surprise answer, as suggested by the above cartoon.

Print answer here

JUMBLE

Unscramble these four Jumbles, one letter to each square, to form four ordinary words.

KLIMY

POCAN

TINADY

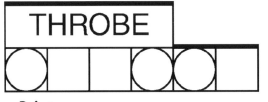

THROBE

It's still not right

Aw, the heck with it

WHEN HE COULDN'T FIX THE VCR CLOCK, HE SAID IT WAS----

Now arrange the circled letters to form the surprise answer, as suggested by the above cartoon.

Print answer here

"◯◯◯◯◯◯◯"

JUMBLE®

Unscramble these four Jumbles, one letter to each square, to form four ordinary words.

NUMOR

CHOAR

MODDEO

SUCLEM

It's only just a...

How DARE you, sir!

ACHOO

THE ARISTOCRAT WAS EMBARRASSED WHEN THE DOCTOR SAID HE HAD----

Now arrange the circled letters to form the surprise answer, as suggested by the above cartoon.

Print answer here A "⬡⬡⬡⬡⬡⬡" ⬡⬡⬡⬡

152

JUMBLE®

Unscramble these four Jumbles, one letter to each square, to form four ordinary words.

ORDOB

BLONE

DEKORF

TSIGAR

Stop, you crook!

WHAT THE POULTRY THIEF DID AT THE GOOSE POND.

Now arrange the circled letters to form the surprise answer, as suggested by the above cartoon.

Print answer here ○○○○ A "○○○○○○"

JUMBLE®

Unscramble these four Jumbles, one letter to each square, to form four ordinary words.

KROJE

RANOB

KHEELS

RERROT

DONE!

It's only been 20 minutes

WHEN HE BROKE THE SPEED-READING RECORD, IT WAS----

Now arrange the circled letters to form the surprise answer, as suggested by the above cartoon.

Print answer here ⬡⬡⬡ FOR ⬡⬡⬡ "⬡⬡⬡⬡⬡⬡"

JUMBLE®

Unscramble these four Jumbles, one letter to each square, to form four ordinary words.

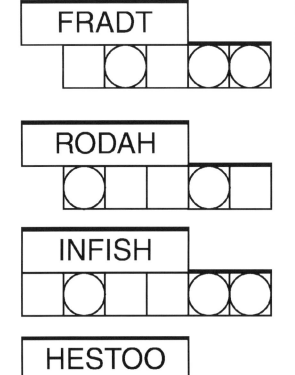

FRADT

RODAH

INFISH

HESTOO

I can't justify even one star

Not for me

WHAT THE FASHION WRITERS GAVE THE LATEST SKIRT LENGTH.

Now arrange the circled letters to form the surprise answer, as suggested by the above cartoon.

Print answer here "⬡⬡⬡⬡⬡⬡" ⬡⬡⬡⬡⬡⬡⬡

JUMBLE®

Unscramble these four Jumbles, one letter to each square, to form four ordinary words.

YOHBB

ROSYR

NIEFED

GURCOH

Ooops!

Look out below

WHEN THE STEEL-WORKER DROPPED THE WATER BOTTLE, HE WAS LEFT----

Now arrange the circled letters to form the surprise answer, as suggested by the above cartoon.

Print answer here ⬡⬡⬡⬡ AND ⬡⬡⬡

156

JUMBLE®

Unscramble these four Jumbles, one letter to each square, to form four ordinary words.

THOOP

CAROK

ENTAUB

ATTARR

I paid $10,000 for this?

WHAT THE HOMEOWNER DID WHEN THE PLUMBER BOTCHED THE REMODELING JOB.

Now arrange the circled letters to form the surprise answer, as suggested by the above cartoon.

Print answer here 〇〇〇〇 A "〇〇〇〇"

JUMBLE®

Unscramble these four Jumbles, one letter to each square, to form four ordinary words.

HAFIT

PODEK

DECAFE

KOOCIE

We won!

HOME 17
VIS. 14

We won!

HOW THE LAST-MINUTE FIELD GOAL AFFECTED THE VICTORY CELEBRATION.

Now arrange the circled letters to form the surprise answer, as suggested by the above cartoon.

Print answer here

IT " ⃝⃝⃝⃝⃝⃝ " IT ⃝⃝⃝

JUMBLE®

Unscramble these four Jumbles, one letter to each square, to form four ordinary words.

BLACE

TEJEC

TORRAM

DISSAT

My portfolio is up 22%

WHAT THE BAKER MADE WHEN THE STOCK MARKET SOARED.

Now arrange the circled letters to form the surprise answer, as suggested by the above cartoon.

Print answer here ⬡⬡⬡⬡ OF " ⬡⬡⬡⬡⬡ "

159

JUMBLE.

Unscramble these four Jumbles, one letter to each square, to form four ordinary words.

TOLCH

NEPEC

NOTINE

MARFOL

Why don't you go catch a crook?

That's it. You're going in

WHERE THE SPEEDER ENDED UP WHEN HE GOT HOT UNDER THE COLLAR.

Now arrange the circled letters to form the surprise answer, as suggested by the above cartoon.

Print answer here IN ⬡⬡⬡ ⬡⬡⬡⬡⬡⬡⬡

PUZZLE 159

JUMBLE®

Unscramble these four Jumbles, one letter to each square, to form four ordinary words.

DULEE

SIZEE

GAMNEA

PREDIM

...and I'm also an expert skydiver...

HOW SHE DESCRIBED HER EGOTISTICAL DATE.

Now arrange the circled letters to form the surprise answer, as suggested by the above cartoon.

Print answer here " ◯◯ " ◯◯◯◯

JUMBLE®

Unscramble these four Jumbles, one letter to each square, to form four ordinary words.

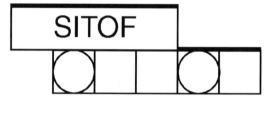

SITOF

YETTS

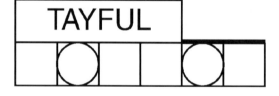

TAYFUL

FAERRY

I've got to lose 10 pounds by tomorrow night

A BOXER WILL DO THIS TO MAKE WEIGHT BEFORE A BIG FIGHT.

Now arrange the circled letters to form the surprise answer, as suggested by the above cartoon.

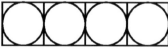

Print answer here A

Juke Joint
JUMBLE®

Challenger

Puzzles

JUMBLE.

Unscramble these six Jumbles, one letter to each square, to form six ordinary words.

DESEEC

PLOGES

EETELY

BAFLLE

YURNEP

DRAISH

M'Lady's

All my clothes were old

I'm down to my last two quarters

MORE FASHION CHANGE CAN LEAD TO THIS.

Now arrange the circled letters to form the surprise answer, as suggested by the above cartoon.

Print answer here

◯◯◯◯ ◯◯◯◯◯ "◯◯◯◯◯◯"

JUMBLE®

Unscramble these six Jumbles, one letter to each square, to form six ordinary words.

HERITH

CRESIB

FLUTIE

STRUMI

NAGUMM

WROFUR

I'm so honored you chose me, Miss Latouse

WHAT THE ARTIST EXPERIENCED WHEN HE DREW THE STAR'S PORTRAIT.

Now arrange the circled letters to form the surprise answer, as suggested by the above cartoon.

Print answer here

A " ◯◯◯◯◯ " ◯◯◯◯ ◯◯◯◯

JUMBLE

Unscramble these six Jumbles, one letter to each square, to form six ordinary words.

JITNEC

THROCC

INYELC

INJOAD

APHERM

POWALL

He thinks he can get away with anything

Where have you been?

On a sales trip, J.B.

HE BECAME A CHRONIC LIAR BECAUSE HE HAD A ---

Now arrange the circled letters to form the surprise answer, as suggested by the above cartoon.

Print answer here

166

JUMBLE®

Unscramble these six Jumbles, one letter to each square, to form six ordinary words.

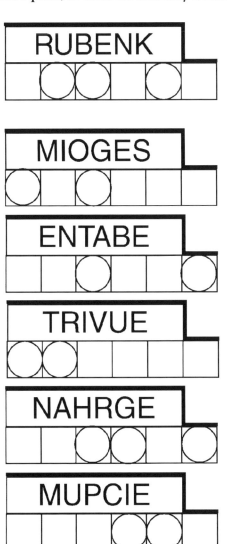

RUBENK

MIOGES

ENTABE

TRIVUE

NAHRGE

MUPCIE

UNFAIR   UNFAIR

She never cooks

He never helps around the house

THE LABOR BOSS AND HIS WIFE GAVE THE MARRIAGE COUN-SELOR A ---

Now arrange the circled letters to form the surprise answer, as suggested by the above cartoon.

Print answer here

"◯◯◯◯◯" ◯◯◯◯◯◯◯◯◯

JUMBLE®

Unscramble these six Jumbles, one letter to each square, to form six ordinary words.

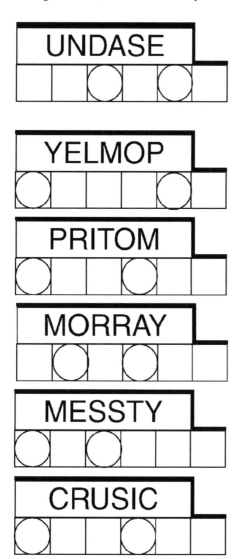

UNDASE

YELMOP

PRITOM

MORRAY

MESSTY

CRUSIC

So soft and fluffy

THE BAKER'S BREAD RECIPE WON THE CONTEST BECAUSE IT---

Now arrange the circled letters to form the surprise answer, as suggested by the above cartoon.

Print answer here

 " ⬡⬡⬡⬡⬡ " TO THE ⬡⬡⬡⬡⬡⬡⬡⬡⬡

168

JUMBLE.

Unscramble these six Jumbles, one letter to
each square, to form six ordinary words.

NUCHAH

NUSIAD

GEELUM

MEENYZ

CLUMON

CINUDE

All is
quiet,
sir

Very well,
carry on

OFF THE
BRITISH COAST,
THE SAILORS
WATCHED THE – – –

Now arrange the circled letters to form the
surprise answer, as suggested by the above
cartoon.

Print answer here

" "

JUMBLE®

Unscramble these six Jumbles, one letter to each square, to form six ordinary words.

NAHDDE

PREFIL

SYMFIL

MOANEY

DROINO

CHOTEL

No, we don't have an itinerary

WHAT THE WAN-
DERING VACATION-
ERS ENJOYED
IN ITALY.

Now arrange the circled letters to form the surprise answer, as suggested by the above cartoon.

Print answer here

A " ⬡⬡⬡⬡⬡⬡ " ⬡⬡⬡⬡⬡⬡⬡

170

JUMBLE®

Unscramble these six Jumbles, one letter to
each square, to form six ordinary words.

VEENEL

GALLOB

MINGOH

NIWWON

SCULIE

CLOMPY

You can
hardly
see it

He didn't
mean it

HARD TO DO
WHEN THE PUPPY
TEARS UP THE
COUCH.

Now arrange the circled letters to form the
surprise answer, as suggested by the above
cartoon.

Print answer here

" ◯◯◯◯◯◯◯ " THE ◯◯◯◯

JUMBLE®

Unscramble these six Jumbles, one letter to
each square, to form six ordinary words.

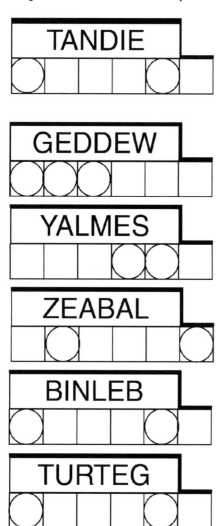

TANDIE

GEDDEW

YALMES

ZEABAL

BINLEB

TURTEG

Y'all sure
look lovely

BONG!

WHEN THEY
STOOD UP AT
THE PLANTA-
TION WEDDING
THEY BECAME---

Now arrange the circled letters to form the
surprise answer, as suggested by the above
cartoon.

Print answer here

172

JUMBLE®

Unscramble these six Jumbles, one letter to each square, to form six ordinary words.

RAHPON

GINPTY

TEENAG

DAUPIN

SHERTH

DOOHKE

Now apply firm pressure on the muscles

WHAT IT TAKES TO BECOME A MASSAGE THERAPIST.

Now arrange the circled letters to form the surprise answer, as suggested by the above cartoon.

Print answer here

◯◯◯◯◯-◯◯ ◯◯◯◯◯◯◯◯◯

MGX Limited went sky high

I told you

WHAT THE SEER
ENJOYED WHEN
SHE INVESTED IN
HER PREDICTION.

JUMBLE

Unscramble these six Jumbles, one letter to each square, to form six ordinary words.

RIMPER

PIGNUM

HURTOF

TRULIA

CROOPE

PHYNOT

Now arrange the circled letters to form the surprise answer, as suggested by the above cartoon.

Print answer here

A ⬡⬡⬡⬡⬡⬡⬡⬡ ⬡⬡⬡⬡⬡⬡

JUMBLE®

Unscramble these six Jumbles, one letter to each square, to form six ordinary words.

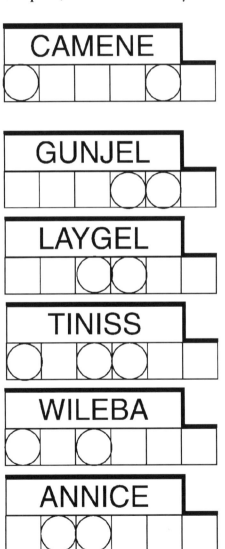

CAMENE

GUNJEL

LAYGEL

TINISS

WILEBA

ANNICE

Muriel, I can't stand this

Just a little more to go

PAINTING THE HOUSE ALL WEEK-END LEFT HIM----

Now arrange the circled letters to form the surprise answer, as suggested by the above cartoon.

Print answer here

JUMBLE®

Unscramble these six Jumbles, one letter to
each square, to form six ordinary words.

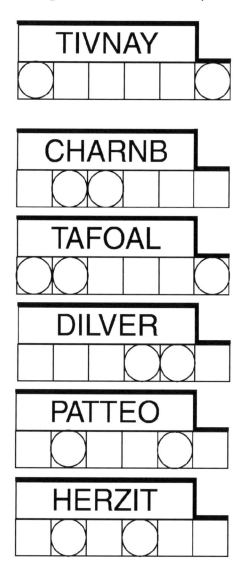

TIVNAY

CHARNB

TAFOAL

DILVER

PATTEO

HERZIT

I took the big
guy for a grand

So did
most of
the others

THE GAMBLER BET
ON THE 300 -
POUND WRESTLER
BECAUSE HE
WAS A---

Now arrange the circled letters to form the
surprise answer, as suggested by the above
cartoon.

Print answer here

JUMBLE®

Unscramble these six Jumbles, one letter to each square, to form six ordinary words.

POOSUR

MILTEY

LAYDED

TOEGEA

DELDUP

DORCEF

SALES OFFICE

He even cleans the tire treads

HIS CARS LOOKED PERFECT BECAUSE HE WAS---

Now arrange the circled letters to form the surprise answer, as suggested by the above cartoon.

Print answer here

◯◯◯◯ WITH " ◯◯◯◯◯◯◯ "

JUMBLE.

Unscramble these six Jumbles, one letter to
each square, to form six ordinary words.

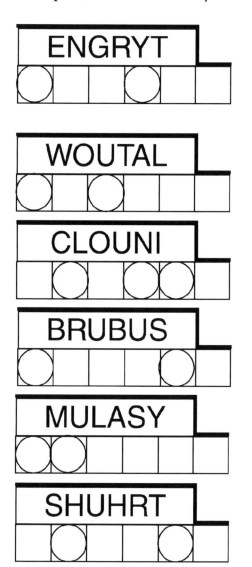

ENGRYT

WOUTAL

CLOUNI

BRUBUS

MULASY

SHUHRT

May I
take your
picture,
Miss La Fame?

WHAT THE ASTRO-
NOMER ENJOYED
WHEN THE CELE-
BRITIES VISITED
THE PLANETARIUM.

Now arrange the circled letters to form the
surprise answer, as suggested by the above
cartoon.

Print answer here

JUMBLE

Unscramble these six Jumbles, one letter to each square, to form six ordinary words.

SLAFTE

CAPALE

TALUCA

PAMEND

CLUDAN

HALTEL

Wow! This baby really moves!

WHEN THE ADMIRAL DROVE THE SPORTS CAR, IT WAS——

Now arrange the circled letters to form the surprise answer, as suggested by the above cartoon.

Print answer here

179

JUMBLE®

Unscramble these six Jumbles, one letter to each square, to form six ordinary words.

STOMED

CLOTEK

PROPHE

NODWIS

CLAIFE

MARROD

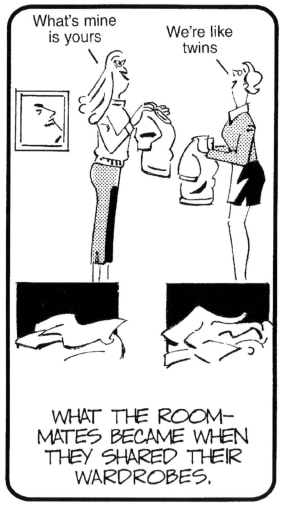

What's mine is yours

We're like twins

WHAT THE ROOM-MATES BECAME WHEN THEY SHARED THEIR WARDROBES.

Now arrange the circled letters to form the surprise answer, as suggested by the above cartoon.

Print answer here

" ◯◯◯◯◯◯◯◯ " ◯◯◯◯◯◯◯◯

JUMBLE®

Unscramble these six Jumbles, one letter to each square, to form six ordinary words.

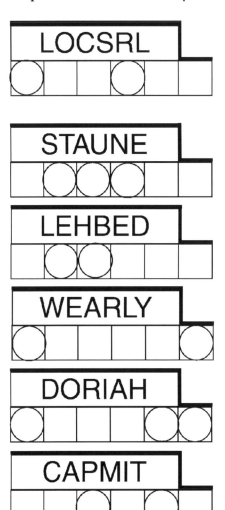

LOCSRL

STAUNE

LEHBED

WEARLY

DORIAH

CAPMIT

I can't stand this music

OFTEN PREFERRED WHEN PUT ON HOLD.

Now arrange the circled letters to form the surprise answer, as suggested by the above cartoon.

Print answer here

A " ⬡⬡⬡⬡⬡-⬡⬡⬡⬡ " ⬡⬡⬡⬡⬡

181

JUMBLE®

Unscramble these six Jumbles, one letter to
each square, to form six ordinary words.

TARREY

RALERY

PLITOE

TULNAW

DIMPEE

GLEMIT

Looks good
enough to
eat

WHAT THE ARTIST
LINKED THROUGH
HIS STILL-LIFE
PAINTING.

Now arrange the circled letters to form the
surprise answer, as suggested by the above
cartoon.

Print answer here

 AND

182

JUMBLE®

Unscramble these six Jumbles, one letter to
each square, to form six ordinary words.

POEQUA

DORWYB

LIGARC

NASTEF

LESPEN

LIEFED

She does
fine work

I don't have
time to eat

WHEN BUSINESS
INCREASED, THE
SEAMSTRESS---

Now arrange the circled letters to form the
surprise answer, as suggested by the above
cartoon.

Print answer here

"◯◯◯◯◯" ◯◯ ◯◯◯◯◯◯◯◯

Answers

1. **Jumbles:** BERET FLAKE BALSAM BUSILY
   Answer: Stale beer can lead to this—"FLAT" SALES

2. **Jumbles:** GAMUT LUSTY ZITHER JUMPER
   Answer: The doc said walking for exercise is—
   THE RIGHT "STEP"

3. **Jumbles:** BERTH WHOOP KOWTOW GOBLET
   Answer: How she finished her gift-wrapping
   demonstration—WITH A BOW BOW

4. **Jumbles:** BLOAT DUNCE TRUSTY HOPPER
   Answer: When the soda truck stalled, traffic was—
   "BOTTLED" UP

5. **Jumbles:** QUEER KNACK FOIBLE UNWISE
   Answer: What the bronco rider ended up getting in the
   rodeo—A FEW "BUCKS"

6. **Jumbles:** VALET THINK VACUUM JAGUAR
   Answer: When the pool hustler appeared on the movie set,
   he was—RIGHT ON "CUE"

7. **Jumbles:** NATAL NOISY POLISH OUTLAW
   Answer: He rode the executive elevator because he
   was—ON HIS WAY "UP"

8. **Jumbles:** SCOUR PLAIT SURTAX FELONY
   Answer: When he apologized for missing curfew, he was in
   a—"SORRY" STATE

9. **Jumbles:** BOOTY GAUGE NOVICE MENACE
   Answer: What he turned into at the masked ball—
   A "BOOGIE" MAN

10. **Jumbles:** LATHE CLOVE FAMILY BICEPS
    Answer: When the hairdresser appeared on TV, his business
    grew at a—FAST "CLIP"

11. **Jumbles:** QUEUE PRUNE VERBAL UNSOLD
    Answer: When he topped the ice cream with hot chili sauce,
    the soda jerk said—"NEVER ON SUNDAE"

12. **Jumbles:** ENSUE FLUTE WISDOM LOCKET
    Answer: Road rage can make this come to a head—
    A FIST OR TWO

13. **Jumbles:** JETTY SHINY FARINA TIMELY
    Answer: When their team lost, the fans were—IN TIERS

14. **Jumbles:** BANDY QUAKE THRIVE LAWYER
    Answer: She dyed her hair because it helped keep her
    age—IN THE "DARK"

15. **Jumbles:** PUTTY CHOKE BAMBOO SUBMIT
    Answer: Where the shoemaker ended up when he joined
    the marines—IN "BOOT" CAMP

16. **Jumbles:** MOUSY OFTEN HOOKUP CALLOW
    Answer: What it takes a harpist to play before an audience—
    LOTS OF PLUCK

17. **Jumbles:** LINEN CHESS POPLIN MINGLE
    Answer: What a couple of busybodies are good at feeding—
    THE GOSSIP MILL

18. **Jumbles:** BAKED PEACE TURNIP BEDECK
    Answer: When he dropped the carton of eggs, his
    coworkers—"CRACKED" UP

19. **Jumbles:** RANCH WEDGE RARELY DRIVEL
    Answer: What hubby did when the ceiling fan needed
    repair—GAVE IT A WHIRL

20. **Jumbles:** VAPOR FEINT CHORUS LETHAL
    Answer: Enjoyed at the Paris eatery—FRENCH "TOAST"

21. **Jumbles:** BATCH SWOON HAZARD WHOLLY
    Answer: When Junior said he didn't sneak a cookie, Mom
    found it was—HARD TO SWALLOW

22. **Jumbles:** ENVOY SLANT CANNED ZINNIA
    Answer: The gambler who went broke lacked this—
    ANY "CENTS"

23. **Jumbles:** LISLE PARCH JINGLE RATHER
    Answer: What he experienced in the low part of the
    ocean—A REAL "HIGH"

24. **Jumbles:** BRAVE JUICY RAMROD DISARM
    Answer: How Mom felt after making jam—"JARRED"

25. **Jumbles:** PIECE DECAY BEHOLD RACIAL
    Answer: What he considered the lovely vendor—
    A REAL "PEACH"

26. **Jumbles:** RABBI NEEDY MODISH VELLUM
    Answer: When the woman pilot got married, her friends said
    she—"LANDED" HIM

27. **Jumbles:** ABIDE MANLY TYRANT COUPLE
    Answer: What she hoped to meet on the singles cruise—
    A "DREAMBOAT"

28. **Jumbles:** TRULY HONOR UNCOIL GENTRY
    Answer: Practiced by the dieting couple—"GIRTH" CONTROL

29. **Jumbles:** DECRY HEFTY SPLICE HITHER
    Answer: When the wildcatters struck oil, they ended
    up—FILTHY, RICH

30. **Jumbles:** MUSIC FLOOD DISMAY TROPHY
    Answer: What the shower turned into when she took too
    much time—A STORM

31. **Jumbles:** IRATE UNCLE GASKET CROUCH
    Answer: The review of royal finances turned out to be
    a—"REIGN" CHECK

32. **Jumbles:** SCARF AWASH HAIRDO ANKLET
    Answer: What the creatures of the deep called the winning
    player—A "CARD SHARK"

33. **Jumbles:** TYPED OPERA MURMUR NOBODY
    Answer: The math team lost the competition because they
    were—"OUTNUMBERED"

34. **Jumbles:** SIXTY SHEAF DENOTE ASSURE
    Answer: When he told them about the whopper, his pals
    said it—"SOUNDS FISHY"

35. **Jumbles:** ABBEY SYNOD NOZZLE HAZING
    Answer: What Mom did when Dad burned the steaks—
    "SIZZLED"

36. **Jumbles:** ACRID NOOSE DISOWN MODEST
    Answer: He finished third in the race because he couldn't
    get his—"SECOND" WIND

37. **Jumbles:** CATCH LEECH UNSEAT FESTAL
    Answer: What the film director did when the movie ran too
    long—CUT TO THE "CHASE"

38. **Jumbles:** APRON BISON TREMOR GAIETY
    Answer: When the teen outlined his homework plans, Mom
    thought it was—"PROMISING"

39. **Jumbles:** NOTCH ANISE IMPACT MISERY
    Answer: The losing stock-car driver was fined for this—
    "RACY" COMMENTS

40. **Jumbles:** THYME FUNNY TINGLE UNFAIR
    Answer: What the family experienced when the barking dog
    kept them awake—A "RUFF" NIGHT

41. **Jumbles:** BILGE EMBER FOSSIL LEDGER
    Answer: She followed in the cover girl's footsteps because
    she wanted—A "MODEL" LIFE

42. **Jumbles:** HOIST LUNGE PICNIC THRUSH
    Answer: Why the headwaiter helped out in the busy
    kitchen—TO STIR THINGS UP

43. **Jumbles:** UTTER ELDER RATIFY SYMBOL
    Answer: What the tuxedo-clad executive dictated to his
    secretary—A "FORMAL" LETTER

44. **Jumbles:** PYLON TEMPO BEHEAD GIMLET
    Answer: When the young kangaroos misbehaved, Mom
    was—"HOPPING" MAD

45. **Jumbles:** CYCLE SURLY LAVISH CHISEL
    Answer: A cold snap can do this to a beach vendor—
    "CHILL" SALES

46. **Jumbles:** EVENT DAILY INDUCT METRIC
    Answer: What the carpenter did when he entered the
    hammering contest—HE "NAILED" IT

47. **Jumbles:** PIETY EXERT PYTHON MARTIN
    Answer: What she spent to buy new makeup—
    A "PRETTY" PENNY

48. **Jumbles:** MOUNT FLORA LOCALE MANIAC
    Answer: Counts when shopping for a car—A CALCULATOR
49. **Jumbles:** NEWLY BANJO CASHEW INLAID
    Answer: The miner quit his job because he was—ALWAYS "DOWN"
50. **Jumbles:** BATON WOMEN MOSQUE OBJECT
    Answer: What Junior's promise turned out to be when the driveway wasn't cleared—A "SNOW" JOB
51. **Jumbles:** DEMON ROBOT COWARD POLITE
    Answer: Suffered by an impatient diner—A "WAIT" PROBLEM
52. **Jumbles:** DAILY HURRY GOBLET VANITY
    Answer: What the judge experienced when he took time off—A "TRYING" DAY
53. **Jumbles:** QUEST CHUTE CHARGE PERMIT
    Answer: When the player married the beauty queen in center field, it was—QUITE A "CATCH"
54. **Jumbles:** NUTTY FRIAR BUSHEL KINDLY
    Answer: The cameraman captured the winning basket—IN A "FLASH"
55. **Jumbles:** COACH MOUND VARIED PEOPLE
    Answer: Important to do when you marry twice—DIVORCE ONCE
56. **Jumbles:** PUPPY JOINT LUNACY AMOEBA
    Answer: What the politician offered the poor fruit peddler—A "PLUM" JOB
57. **Jumbles:** ADMIT CREEK DAMPEN STICKY
    Answer: What the doctor's diagnosis did to the hypochondriac—MADE HIM SICK
58. **Jumbles:** OAKEN ADULT WAITER SPLEEN
    Answer: What he wanted to do when he settled up with his ex-wife—SETTLE DOWN
59. **Jumbles:** PATIO TASTY ENSIGN HERESY
    Answer: What the boss did when the highway striper wasn't careful—SET HIM "STRAIGHT"
60. **Jumbles:** BEFOG SHYLY BANISH ESTATE
    Answer: When the latest style sandals were introduced they were bound to be—A SHOE-IN
61. **Jumbles:** KNAVE SNACK STANZA APPALL
    Answer: What sleeping bags can turn into on the spur of the moment—"NAP" SACKS
62. **Jumbles:** RUSTY QUEEN DETACH BASKET
    Answer: When the cops demanded the bare facts, they got—THE NAKED TRUTH
63. **Jumbles:** GUILD UNITY NUANCE HANSOM
    Answer: How the builder reacted when the door was the wrong size—HE GOT UNHINGED
64. **Jumbles:** PRIME INEPT SPORTY BEMOAN
    Answer: What she earned by selling her handmade brooches—"PIN" MONEY
65. **Jumbles:** PRINT JERKY INDICT OPIATE
    Answer: Where the teenager ended up when he spilled the drink—ON THE CARPET
66. **Jumbles:** FAMED AUGUR HICCUP CONCUR
    Answer: A hug for hubby after a shopping trip is a good way to get—"AROUND" HIM
67. **Jumbles:** GUMMY DAISY STIGMA BANGLE
    Answer: What the switchboard operator gave her boss—A "BUSY" SIGNAL
68. **Jumbles:** DINER OUTDO ALIGHT REFUGE
    Answer: Who did Dracula take to the Halloween party?—A "GHOUL" FRIEND
69. **Jumbles:** WALTZ TAFFY VELVET SUPERB
    Answer: Encountered in the old print shop—ALL "TYPES"
70. **Jumbles:** PARKA ALIVE ABACUS EXPEND
    Answer: The janitor's favorite spot in the batting order—CLEANUP
71. **Jumbles:** ABHOR ENEMY AGENCY DEVOUR
    Answer: Why the shipwrecked sailor turned purple with rage—HE WAS "MAROONED"
72. **Jumbles:** RIVET AFIRE HANGAR GROTTO
    Answer: The geology student flunked his rocks exam because he took—IT FOR "GRANITE"
73. **Jumbles:** WHEEL GLADE EFFIGY NUDISM
    Answer: Why they were attracted to the sprinter—HE WAS "DASHING"
74. **Jumbles:** STOOP CRUSH FOURTH DEVICE
    Answer: When he took his ex-girl's bridal photos, he was—OUT OF THE PICTURE
75. **Jumbles:** CANAL LINGO GAMBLE CAUCUS
    Answer: How the food critic described his job—ALL "CONSUMING"
76. **Jumbles:** WINCE TRUTH POTENT VIOLIN
    Answer: What the comedian gave the heckler—A "PUNCH" LINE
77. **Jumbles:** FILMY MANGY PROFIT QUAVER
    Answer: What she kept in her makeup case—"VANITY" FARE
78. **Jumbles:** PROXY BLOOM JARGON FAMOUS
    Answer: Developed by the gifted minor-league player—"MAJOR" PLANS
79. **Jumbles:** LARVA GIVEN SIZZLE PODIUM
    Answer: What she considered his introduction at the singles bar—AN "I" OPENER
80. **Jumbles:** CEASE BEFIT LADING NOTIFY
    Answer: When the tabby cuddled on her lap, she was—"FELINE" FINE
81. **Jumbles:** LYRIC KHAKI WEDGED AVOWAL
    Answer: What the pitcher did when he couldn't throw a strike—"WALKED" AWAY
82. **Jumbles:** TITLE BOWER RABBIT BEAUTY
    Answer: He took blackjack lessons to become—A BETTER BETTOR
83. **Jumbles:** BARGE TULLE HERMIT VACANT
    Answer: Shoddy work will do this to a tailor's sales—UNRAVEL THEM
84. **Jumbles:** PAGAN SWISH ELICIT BANDIT
    Answer: The kind of headache a divorce can cause—"SPLITTING"
85. **Jumbles:** VITAL BANAL UNLESS AIRWAY
    Answer: Why she sought new fabric for the well-used easy chair—IT WAS "SAT-IN"
86. **Jumbles:** CHAIR METAL HEIFER CURFEW
    Answer: What the town hoped for during the annual carnival days—"FAIR" WEATHER
87. **Jumbles:** SWOOP POISE EXOTIC CLOUDY
    Answer: Important for a roof garden—"TOP" SOIL
88. **Jumbles:** SAVOR UNWED DONKEY QUIVER
    Answer: What the neighbors did about the noisy parrots—"SQUAWKED"
89. **Jumbles:** ABBOT ELITE LIMPID RENDER
    Answer: He became a champion racer by putting his—"METTLE" TO THE PEDAL
90. **Jumbles:** TRYST OCCUR INVOKE PAUPER
    Answer: When the boaters landed in the middle of the lake, they were—UP THE CREEK
91. **Jumbles:** BLESS FRAUD MISFIT BESIDE
    Answer: The turkey and the family were this on Thanksgiving—"STUFFED"
92. **Jumbles:** BELIE LIMBO EXTANT FROZEN
    Answer: When the vegetarian yelled at the server, he had a—REAL "BEEF"
93. **Jumbles:** REARM ARDOR ANYHOW VALUED
    Answer: The helper didn't laugh at the roofer's joke because it was—OVER HIS HEAD
94. **Jumbles:** BRINY SINGE MYOPIC TIMING
    Answer: She gave him a good-night kiss because he seemed—"PROMISING"
95. **Jumbles:** KETCH CRACK DAMASK RANCID
    Answer: Harder to deal with after a while—A DECK OF CARDS

96. **Jumbles:** WEIGH MESSY PITIED TANKER
Answer: After eating all that chocolate, Junior fell asleep and had—"SWEET" DREAMS

97. **Jumbles:** DOWNY SOOTY ADAGIO ORIOLE
Answer: Stressed in a penmanship class—DOING IT "WRITE"

98. **Jumbles:** HEDGE LIGHT PURITY OMELET
Answer: What the judge did to the phone thief—PUT HIM ON "HOLD"

99. **Jumbles:** GUESS ENACT THWART BARIUM
Answer: What the picnickers formed to battle the insects—A "SWAT" TEAM

100. **Jumbles:** VIGIL AGILE GIGGLE FAMISH
Answer: When he kept repeating the old jokes, the host wanted to—GIVE HIM A "GAG"

101. **Jumbles:** AIDED TOXIN BELLOW FABLED
Answer: What the banker did—FLOATED "ALONE"

102. **Jumbles:** NUDGE TOXIC JUSTLY PETITE
Answer: What the couple did when they couldn't decide on a mattress—"SLEPT" ON IT

103. **Jumbles:** PAPER ANKLE RAGLAN CRABBY
Answer: She didn't buy the bikini because she couldn't—BEAR TO BARE

104. **Jumbles:** TOOTH POACH VOLUME TANGLE
Answer: A hammock is a good place to do this on a summer day—"HANG" OUT

105. **Jumbles:** LYING BULGY GOVERN INCOME
Answer: The lumberjack's favorite task on a computer—"LOGGING" ON

106. **Jumbles:** IDIOT TEPID PRYING TWINGE
Answer: When the couple exchanged vows in the pool, they were—"RINGING" WET

107. **Jumbles:** BLIMP JUDGE WAYLAY BAUBLE
Answer: What she said when she quit shopping to save money—BYE BUY

108. **Jumbles:** LILAC BASSO AUTHOR BEHALF
Answer: Why the shy wife wanted to go home from the party—SHE WAS "BASH" FULL

109. **Jumbles:** PUDGY SAUTE FABRIC WHEEZE
Answer: What the chief of the accounting staff was known as—A "FIGURE" HEAD

110. **Jumbles:** HARDY IMBUE MALLET PUSHER
Answer: Why the tailors hired the young apprentice—HE "MEASURED" UP

111. **Jumbles:** GUMBO CARGO PUZZLE JESTER
Answer: What the rival executives discussed when they fell in love—THE URGE TO MERGE

112. **Jumbles:** TRILL YOKEL POISON WEAKEN
Answer: These headlines can upset an aging fashion editor—WRINKLES

113. **Jumbles:** YACHT ORBIT SICKEN VISION
Answer: When Mom watched the sitcom while hemming a skirt, she was—IN "STITCHES"

114. **Jumbles:** ROUSE WIPED CATCHY INFECT
Answer: What the sailors liked best during their leave overseas—IT WAS "DUTY" FREE

115. **Jumbles:** DUSKY BOUGH SALOON BOILED
Answer: Why the beauty queen became a spy—SHE "LOOKED" GOOD

116. **Jumbles:** NOISE FOYER WOEFUL EFFORT
Answer: The cops caught the pickpocket with quick hands because of this—SLOW FEET

117. **Jumbles:** SANDY DERBY BOUGHT INTACT
Answer: What the office worker said when he rushed outside for a smoke—IT'S A "DRAG"

118. **Jumbles:** KINKY BALMY ENJOIN IMBIBE
Answer: A quarterback can turn into this on the bench—A "LINE" MAN

119. **Jumbles:** DUCHY LOFTY GUIDED CRAVAT
Answer: What the couple did when the carpeting was installed—CUT A RUG

120. **Jumbles:** CRAZE SHEEP LIQUOR PELVIS
Answer: The upholsterer said the chains on his tires were—"SLIP" COVERS

121. **Jumbles:** HITCH TRAIT GAMBIT FORGET
Answer: What the barflies resorted to when they had an argument—A "TIGHT" FIGHT

122. **Jumbles:** GRIPE COLON PIRACY GADFLY
Answer: This can be harder than a diamond—PAYING FOR IT

123. **Jumbles:** SCARY GUIDE LANCER HYMNAL
Answer: What the clown looked like when he dressed for his big date—A "CHANGED" MAN

124. **Jumbles:** DEITY POWER OBLIGE TURTLE
Answer: How the napkin salesman felt at the end of the day—"WIPED" OUT

125. **Jumbles:** FOCUS VILLA SUBTLY PONCHO
Answer: What it can cost to go after big bucks—LOTS OF CASH

126. **Jumbles:** FEWER RAVEN CABANA ADMIRE
Answer: His family looked on proudly because the baker was their—"BREADWINNER"

127. **Jumbles:** MERGE FORAY MAMMAL TOWARD
Answer: What the travel agent wanted the pesky customer to do—GO AWAY

128. **Jumbles:** FISHY ROBIN SIPHON POETIC
Answer: When he developed the portrait of the racehorse, it was a—PHOTO "FINISH"

129. **Jumbles:** GNARL LITHE SOCIAL ACCORD
Answer: He became a fisherman because it was—"CATCHING"

130. **Jumbles:** WHINE FABLE EIGHTY GENTLE
Answer: The drapery helper was fired because he couldn't—GET THE "HANG" OF IT

131. **Jumbles:** CUBIC RAINY PAYOFF SPONGE
Answer: What a bettor has to do when his horse loses the race—"PONY" UP

132. **Jumbles:** DANDY ARMOR JOYFUL ENGULF
Answer: When he was acquitted, the defendant said he had—A "GRAND" JURY

133. **Jumbles:** FENCE HUMAN NAUGHT BUMPER
Answer: A novice gardener is sure to have this—A "GREEN" THUMB

134. **Jumbles:** WAFER USURY CLERGY MYSTIC
Answer: What the ship's barber gave the sailors—"CREW" CUTS

135. **Jumbles:** PLUME HAIRY KIDNAP MOTIVE
Answer: Rain can do this to picnic plans—"DAMPEN" THEM

136. **Jumbles:** EXTOL CAMEO HIDING LEEWAY
Answer: When the trout weren't biting, the fishermen had to—"WADE" FOR THEM

137. **Jumbles:** GULLY HELLO JOBBER BEDBUG
Answer: What the king did when the castle was remodeled—HE "RULED"

138. **Jumbles:** FAULT APART STUCCO POORLY
Answer: Why the tennis champ played a match with the judge—TO COURT THE COURT

139. **Jumbles:** SNARL ERUPT MADMAN JIGGER
Answer: What a photographer needs when shooting a sports event—"SNAP" JUDGMENT

140. **Jumbles:** INLET GASSY RADIUS SHOULD
Answer: She threw away the cookbook because it was—HARD TO "DIGEST"

141. **Jumbles:** SIEGE COUGH UPSHOT HELIUM
Answer: What the pole vaulter had before the competition—"HIGH" HOPES

142. **Jumbles:** GUILT TABOO MEMORY BEHIND
Answer: What the zookeeper turned into every weekend—A "GAME" HUNTER

143. **Jumbles:** BATHE TWEAK STRONG TRYING
Answer: When she bought her cruise wear, she made sure it was—"SEE" WORTHY

144. **Jumbles:** BEGOT TARRY SINFUL HOURLY
Answer: What the king received for his autobiography—
"ROYAL-TIES"

145. **Jumbles:** MERCY MIRTH DULCET GALAXY
Answer: How Grandpa felt when the kids listened to rap music—"EAR-ITATED"

146. **Jumbles:** FORTY TIGER BUTTER ATOMIC
Answer: What the beauty queen wore when she greeted the winning driver—A "RACY" OUTFIT

147. **Jumbles:** BRAVO ICILY PAROLE HECKLE
Answer: Where the student ended up when he completed the sailing course—AT "C" LEVEL

148. **Jumbles:** LATCH HIKER ENTAIL THRASH
Answer: The barflies got sick because they imbibed too often to—THEIR HEALTH

149. **Jumbles:** MILKY CAPON DAINTY BOTHER
Answer: When he couldn't fix the VCR clock, he said it was—ON THE "BLINK"

150. **Jumbles:** MOURN ROACH DOOMED MUSCLE
Answer: The aristocrat was embarrassed when the doctor said he had—A "COMMON" COLD

151. **Jumbles:** BROOD NOBLE FORKED GRATIS
Answer: What the poultry thief did at the goose pond—TOOK A "GANDER"

152. **Jumbles:** JOKER BARON SHEKEL TERROR
Answer: When he broke the speed-reading record, it was—ONE FOR THE "BOOKS"

153. **Jumbles:** DRAFT HOARD FINISH SOOTHE
Answer: What the fashion writers gave the latest skirt length—"SHORT" SHRIFT

154. **Jumbles:** HOBBY SORRY DEFINE GROUCH
Answer: When the steelworker dropped the water bottle, he was left—HIGH AND DRY

155. **Jumbles:** PHOTO CROAK BUTANE TARTAR
Answer: What the homeowner did when the plumber botched the remodeling job—TOOK A "BATH"

156. **Jumbles:** FAITH POKED DEFACE COOKIE
Answer: How the last-minute field goal affected the victory celebration—IT "KICKED" IT OFF

157. **Jumbles:** CABLE EJECT MORTAR SADIST
Answer: What the baker made when the stock market soared—LOTS OF "BREAD"

158. **Jumbles:** CLOTH PENCE INTONE FORMAL
Answer: Where the speeder ended up when he got hot under the collar—IN THE COOLER

159. **Jumbles:** ELUDE SEIZE MANAGE PRIMED
Answer: How she described her egotistical date—"ME" DEEP

160. **Jumbles:** FOIST TESTY FAULTY RAREFY
Answer: A boxer will do this to make weight before a big fight—A FAST FAST

161. **Jumbles:** SECEDE GOSPEL EYELET BEFALL PENURY RADISH
Answer: More fashion change can lead to this—LESS REAL "CHANGE"

162. **Jumbles:** HITHER SCRIBE FUTILE TRUISM MAGNUM FURROW
Answer: What the artist experienced when he drew the star's portrait—A "BRUSH" WITH FAME

163. **Jumbles:** INJECT CROTCH NICELY ADJOIN HAMPER WALLOP
Answer: He became a chronic liar because he had a—MYTH CONCEPTION

164. **Jumbles:** BUNKER EGOISM BEATEN VIRTUE HANGER PUMICE
Answer: The labor boss and his wife gave the marriage counselor a—"UNION" GRIEVANCE

165. **Jumbles:** SUNDAE EMPLOY IMPORT ARMORY SYSTEM CIRCUS
Answer: The baker's bread recipe won the contest because it—"ROSE" TO THE OCCASION

166. **Jumbles:** HAUNCH UNSAID LEGUME ENZYME COLUMN INDUCE
Answer: Off the British coast, the sailors watched the—ENGLISH "CHANNEL"

167. **Jumbles:** HANDED PILFER FLIMSY YEOMAN INDOOR CLOTHE
Answer: What the wandering vacationers enjoyed in Italy—A "ROAMIN'" HOLIDAY

168. **Jumbles:** ELEVEN GLOBAL HOMING WINNOW SLUICE COMPLY
Answer: Hard to do when the puppy tears up the couch—"CUSHION" THE BLOW

169. **Jumbles:** DETAIN WEDGED MEASLY ABLAZE NIBBLE GUTTER
Answer: When they stood up at the plantation wedding they became—WEDDING BELLES

170. **Jumbles:** ORPHAN TYPING NEGATE UNPAID THRESH HOOKED
Answer: What it takes to become a massage therapist—HANDS-ON TRAINING

171. **Jumbles:** PRIMER IMPUGN FOURTH RITUAL COOPER PYTHON
Answer: What the seer enjoyed when she invested in her prediction—A PROPHET PROFIT

172. **Jumbles:** MENACE JUNGLE GALLEY INSIST BEWAIL CANINE
Answer: Painting the house all weekend left him—CLIMBING WALLS

173. **Jumbles:** VANITY BRANCH AFLOAT DRIVEL TEAPOT ZITHER
Answer: The gambler bet on the 300-pound wrestler because he was a—"HEAVY" FAVORITE

174. **Jumbles:** POROUS TIMELY DEADLY GOATEE PUDDLE FORCED
Answer: His cars looked perfect because he was—GOOD WITH "DETAILS"

175. **Jumbles:** GENTRY OUTLAW UNCOIL SUBURB ASYLUM THRUSH
Answer: What the astronomer enjoyed when the celebrities visited the planetarium—SHOOTING "STARS"

176. **Jumbles:** FESTAL PALACE ACTUAL DAMPEN UNCLAD LETHAL
Answer: When the admiral drove the sports car, it was—FULL SPEED AHEAD

177. **Jumbles:** MODEST LOCKET HOPPER DISOWN FACILE RAMROD
Answer: What the roommates became when they shared their wardrobes—"CLOTHES" FRIENDS

178. **Jumbles:** SCROLL UNSEAT BEHELD LAWYER HAIRDO IMPACT
Answer: Often preferred when put on hold—A "CHORD-LESS" PHONE

179. **Jumbles:** ARTERY RARELY POLITE WALNUT IMPEDE GIMLET
Answer: What the artist linked through his still-life painting—PALATE AND PALETTE

180. **Jumbles:** OPAQUE BYWORD GARLIC FASTEN SPLEEN DEFILE
Answer: When business increased, the seamstress—"SEWED" UP PROFITS

187

Need More Jumbles®?

Order any of these books through your bookseller or call Triumph Books toll-free at 800-335-5323.

Jumble® Books

More than 175 puzzles each!

Cowboy Jumble®
ISBN: 978-1-62937-355-3

Jammin' Jumble®
ISBN: 1-57243-844-4

Java Jumble®
ISBN: 978-1-60078-415-6

Jazzy Jumble®
ISBN: 978-1-57243-962-7

Jet Set Jumble®
ISBN: 978-1-60078-353-1

Joyful Jumble®
ISBN: 978-1-60078-079-0

Juke Joint Jumble®
ISBN: 978-1-60078-295-4

Jumble® Anniversary
ISBN: 987-1-62937-734-6

Jumble® at Work
ISBN: 1-57243-147-4

Jumble® Ballet
ISBN: 978-1-62937-616-5

Jumble® Birthday
ISBN: 978-1-62937-652-3

Jumble® Celebration
ISBN: 978-1-60078-134-6

Jumble® Circus
ISBN: 978-1-60078-739-3

Jumble® Cuisine
ISBN: 978-1-62937-735-3

Jumble® Drag Race
ISBN: 978-1-62937-483-3

Jumble® Ever After
ISBN: 978-1-62937-785-8

Jumble® Explorer
ISBN: 978-1-60078-854-3

Jumble® Explosion
ISBN: 978-1-60078-078-3

Jumble® Fever
ISBN: 1-57243-593-3

Jumble® Fiesta
ISBN: 1-57243-626-3

Jumble® Fun
ISBN: 1-57243-379-5

Jumble® Galaxy
ISBN: 978-1-60078-583-2

Jumble® Garden
ISBN: 978-1-62937-653-0

Jumble® Genius
ISBN: 1-57243-896-7

Jumble® Geography
ISBN: 978-1-62937-615-8

Jumble® Getaway
ISBN: 978-1-60078-547-4

Jumble® Gold
ISBN: 978-1-62937-354-6

Jumble® Grab Bag
ISBN: 1-57243-273-X

Jumble® Gymnastics
ISBN: 978-1-62937-306-5

Jumble® Jackpot
ISBN: 1-57243-897-5

Jumble® Jailbreak
ISBN: 978-1-62937-002-6

Jumble® Jambalaya
ISBN: 978-1-60078-294-7

Jumble® Jamboree
ISBN: 1-57243-696-4

Jumble® Jitterbug
ISBN: 978-1-60078-584-9

Jumble® Journey
ISBN: 978-1-62937-549-6

Jumble® Jubilation
ISBN: 978-1-62937-784-1

Jumble® Jubilee
ISBN: 1-57243-231-4

Jumble® Juggernaut
ISBN: 978-1-60078-026-4

Jumble® Junction
ISBN: 1-57243-380-9

Jumble® Jungle
ISBN: 978-1-57243-961-0

Jumble® Kingdom
ISBN: 978-1-62937-079-8

Jumble® Knockout
ISBN: 978-1-62937-078-1

Jumble® Madness
ISBN: 1-892049-24-4

Jumble® Magic
ISBN: 978-1-60078-795-9

Jumble® Marathon
ISBN: 978-1-60078-944-1

Jumble® Neighbor
ISBN: 978-1-62937-845-9

Jumble® Parachute
ISBN: 978-1-62937-548-9

Jumble® Safari
ISBN: 978-1-60078-675-4

Jumble® See & Search
ISBN: 1-57243-549-6

Jumble® See & Search 2
ISBN: 1-57243-734-0

Jumble® Sensation
ISBN: 978-1-60078-548-1

Jumble® Surprise
ISBN: 1-57243-320-5

Jumble® Symphony
ISBN: 978-1-62937-131-3

Jumble® Theater
ISBN: 978-1-62937-484-03

Jumble® University
ISBN: 978-1-62937-001-9

Jumble® Unleashed
ISBN: 978-1-62937-844-2

Jumble® Vacation
ISBN: 978-1-60078-796-6

Jumble® Wedding
ISBN: 978-1-62937-307-2

Jumble® Workout
ISBN: 978-1-60078-943-4

Jumpin' Jumble®
ISBN: 978-1-60078-027-1

Lunar Jumble®
ISBN: 978-1-60078-853-6

Monster Jumble®
ISBN: 978-1-62937-213-6

Mystic Jumble®
ISBN: 978-1-62937-130-6

Outer Space Jumble®
ISBN: 978-1-60078-416-3

Rainy Day Jumble®
ISBN: 978-1-60078-352-4

Ready, Set, Jumble®
ISBN: 978-1-60078-133-0

Rock 'n' Roll Jumble®
ISBN: 978-1-60078-674-7

Royal Jumble®
ISBN: 978-1-60078-738-6

Sports Jumble®
ISBN: 1-57243-113-X

Summer Fun Jumble®
ISBN: 1-57243-114-8

Touchdown Jumble®
ISBN: 978-1-62937-212-9

Travel Jumble®
ISBN: 1-57243-198-9

TV Jumble®
ISBN: 1-57243-461-9

Oversize Jumble® Books

More than 500 puzzles each!

Generous Jumble®
ISBN: 1-57243-385-X

Giant Jumble®
ISBN: 1-57243-349-3

Gigantic Jumble®
ISBN: 1-57243-426-0

Jumbo Jumble®
ISBN: 1-57243-314-0

The Very Best of Jumble® BrainBusters
ISBN: 1-57243-845-2

Jumble® Crosswords

More than 175 puzzles each!

More Jumble® Crosswords™
ISBN: 1-57243-386-8

Jumble® Crosswords™ Jackpot
ISBN: 1-57243-615-8

Jumble® Crosswords™ Jamboree
ISBN: 1-57243-787-1

Jumble® BrainBusters™

More than 175 puzzles each!

Jumble® BrainBusters™
ISBN: 1-892049-28-7

Jumble® BrainBusters™ II
ISBN: 1-57243-424-4

Jumble® BrainBusters™ III
ISBN: 1-57243-463-5

Jumble® BrainBusters™ IV
ISBN: 1-57243-489-9

Jumble® BrainBusters™ 5
ISBN: 1-57243-548-8

Jumble® BrainBusters™ Bonanza
ISBN: 1-57243-616-6

Boggle™ BrainBusters™
ISBN: 1-57243-592-5

Boggle™ BrainBusters™ 2
ISBN: 1-57243-788-X

Jumble® BrainBusters™ Junior
ISBN: 1-892049-29-5

Jumble® BrainBusters™ Junior II
ISBN: 1-57243-425-2

Fun in the Sun with Jumble® BrainBusters™
ISBN: 1-57243-733-2